SIXTEEN NEW TESTAMENT MYSTERIES

SIXTEEN NEW TESTAMENT MYSTERIES

MYSTERIES

The Deep things of God

Tommy L. Jamison

XULON PRESS

Xulon Press
2301 Lucien Way #415
Maitland, FL 32751
407.339.4217
www.xulonpress.com

Unless otherwise indicated, Scripture quotations taken from the King James Version (KJV)–*public domain.*

Paperback ISBN-13: 978-1-6628-3543-8
Ebook ISBN-13: 978-1-6628-3544-5

Table of Contents

Preface

Throughout history, future events and circumstances have been revealed to God's people. The primary conveyor in the Old Testament of things revealed was through the prophets of God. God completed His plan, will and Word to mankind through the Spirit-filled writers of the New Testament. However, found in the New Testament are multiple mysteries whereby God's truths are revealed through an understanding of what God meant by mysteries, such as "The mystery of Israel's blindness," "The mystery of Christ," "The mystery of the kingdom of heaven," and "The mystery of iniquity." What did God mean by mystery? What was the purpose of God's mysteries? How can one grasp the meaning of the mysteries?

Mystery in the Greek is *musterion* (ανστηρτον). "In the New Testament it denotes, not the mysterious, but that which, being outside the range of unassisted natural apprehension, can be made known only by Divine revelation and is made known in a manner and at a time appointed by God, and to those only who are illumined by His Spirit."[1] The significance is that truth is revealed. The truth is there for the believer to understand as they desire the meat of God's Word. A casual approach to studying God's Word will not reveal many of these truths. An admonition is made clear concerning spiritual growth whereby the Holy Spirit reveals more and more to the believer in Hebrews 5:12–14:

---

[1]   W.E. Vine, *An Expository Dictionary of New Testament Words* 1966, Fleming H. Revell Company, Old Tappan, New Jersey. **A**

"For when for the time ye ought to be teachers, ye have need that one teach you again which be the first principles of the oracles of God; and are become such as have need of milk, and not of strong meat. For every one that useth milk is unskillful in the word of righteousness: for he is a babe. But strong meat belongeth to them that are of full age, even those who by reason of use have their senses exercised to discern both good and evil."

The mysteries are clearly meat of the Word of God and should be desired for growth as a believer. Paul said in 1 Corinthians 4:1–2, "Let a man so account of us, as of ministers of Christ, and stewards of the mysteries of God. Moreover, it is required in stewards, that a man be found faithful." So, who are the ministers and stewards of the mysteries of God that Paul is calling on? The Greek word that Paul used for minister is *huperetes* (ὑπηρέτης), meaning any subordinate acting under the direction of a superior. It was used to signify the attendant at the synagogue service.[2] Christ is the believer's superior. The Greek word Paul used for steward is *oikonomos* (οἰκονόμος), meaning preachers of the gospel, teachers of the Word of God, elders and bishops of churches, and believers in general.[3] Christ is every believer's superior, and every believer is to be a good steward of the mysteries of God. To be competent in anything, a person must know the subject. To be a good steward of the mysteries of God, the person must know and understand the mysteries. Are most Christians found faithful because their knowledge and understanding of the Word allow them to be good stewards of God's mysteries?

---

[2]   Ibid.

[3]   Ibid.

In the apostle Peter's second epistle, he encourages believers to be diligent in looking and preparing for the day of the Lord. Peter references the wisdom given to his beloved brother Paul who had written in all his epistles the things God had revealed. Concerning Paul's epistles, Peter sates that: "in which are some things hard to be understood, which they thar are unlearned and unstable wrest, as they do also the other scriptures, unto their own destruction." (2 Peter 3:16). Of the sixteen mysteries revealed in the New Testament, Paul provides the insight into ten of them. Therefore, those that study these mysteries should be aware as Peter warned, some things are hard to understand. More than reading is required. Study is mandatory!

The objective of this book is to provide a list of those mysteries spoken of in the Bible while placing in context the order of the mysteries and the truths they reveal. For example, the mystery of the Church was not revealed to the Old Testament saints. When Daniel sought to understand what God had in store for the nation of Israel, he was given a time line of seventy weeks of years, but the time of the Church age was not revealed to Daniel.

Each mystery is presented so that it can be studied as a standalone. However, by following the sequence presented, more clarity of context is provided. Each chapter is preceded by an outline. The outline provides scripture and overview for the student to contemplate prior to studying the written chapter.

Chapter 1

The Mystery of Christ

Jesus Christ, a Hidden Mystery

Ephesians 3:4–5; Colossians 4:3; Colossians 1:24–29

I. **Context: Mysteries hidden from past ages. (Eph. 3:1–12)**

> ➤ The mystery of Christ not made known unto the sons of men.
> ➤ The fellowship of the mystery hidden from principalities and powers.

II. **Christ the Messiah was not hidden?**

- Prophesied by Isaiah as the Child born called "Wonderful, Counselor, The Mighty God, The Everlasting Father, The Prince of Peace" (Isa. 9:6–7). "Unto you is born a savior, Christ the Lord" (Luke 2:8–14).
- Prophecy of the Herald of the Messiah, John the Baptist. (Isa. 40:3–5; Luke 3:3–6 "A voice crying in the wilderness").
- Prophesied by Isaiah as the Suffering Servant. (Isa. 2:14; 50:6–7; 52:13–14; Zechariah 12:10; John19:1–3).
- Rejected by the Jews (Isa. 53:3). He was despised and rejected (Luke 19:39–40).

- Crucified for our sin (Isa. 53:7–9,10–12). His soul made an offering for Sin (John 19:16–18, 30; Matt. 27:35).
- Messiah the Prince was cut off. (Dan. 9:25).
- Raised from the dead (Ps. 16:10; Matt. 28:35).
- Therefore, Messiah was not hidden from either the Old Testament Jews nor the New Testament Jews.

III. The Difference between Old Testament Saints and New Testament Saints

1. Means of forgiveness: Animal sacrifice a sin offering (Lev 4, 6, for an individual sinner, conducted by a priest) versus Christ's once-for-all sacrifice. (Heb. 9:12, 26).

2. Sins forgiven in the Old Testament: the priest made an atonement for the person (Lev. 6:7; Heb. 10:11). Forgiven in the New Testament, one sacrifice for all sin, forever. (Heb. 10:12; 1 John 1:9).

   The Old Testament saints remained in Sheol, hence Paradise or Abraham's bosom (Ps. 68:18; 1 Sam. 28:11–15). Samuel brought up, (Luke 16:23). The New Testament Saint's soul goes immediately to heaven, (2 Cor. 5:8).

3. Old Testament saints are not the bride of Christ. John the Baptist was the friend of the Bridegroom (John 3:39). For New Testament saints, the Church is the bride (Rev. 19:7–9; called to the marriage supper of the Lamb are Old Testament saints, Rev. 21:9–10).

4. The greatest difference is between the Old Testament and New Testament believer is "Christ in you the hope of glory" (Col. 1:27).

IV. Christ in You the Hope of Glory Was Hidden (Col. 1:24–29).

1. The Spirit of Jesus Christ (the Holy Spirit) indwelled Paul (Phil. 1:19–21).
2. The Comforter (the Holy Spirit) promised to indwell all believers during the Church age (John 16:7, 13–14; 14:17).
3. The Holy Spirit's activities during the Old and New Testament (Judg. 15:14, 1 Sam. 10:6; Ezek. 2:2; Acts 4:31).

The Mystery of Christ
Ephesians 3:4–5; Colossians 1:24–29; 4:3

I. Context: In Ephesians 3:1–12, two mysteries are introduced. Some commentators introduce the mystery of Christ (v. 3) and the fellowship of the mystery (v. 9) as simply the mystery of the Church. However, when speaking of the mystery of Christ, Paul said in verses 3–6:

> "How that by revelation he made known unto me the mystery (as I wrote before in few words, By which when ye read, ye may understand my knowledge in the *mystery of Christ*) Which in other ages was not made known unto the *sons of men* as it is now revealed unto his holy apostles and prophets by the Spirit: That the Gentiles should be fellow heirs, and of the same body and partakers of his promise in Christ by the gospel."

> Paul had a great desire to share the mystery of Christ as his words to the Colossians indicate: "Praying also for us, that God would open unto us a door of utterance, to speak the mystery of Christ, for which I am also in bonds" (Col. 4:3). The Holy Spirit had opened Paul's eyes to great spiritual truths and he had a great desire to share them.

What was the mystery that was now being revealed to Paul and the other apostles concerning Jesus Christ? It is that both Jew and Gentile would be fellow heirs of salvation by the Spirit of Christ Jesus (the Holy Spirit) dwelling in the believers. In other ages, the mystery of Christ had not been fully revealed to the sons of men because the Holy Spirit did not indwell all believers. A great revelation of the mystery of Christ happened at Pentecost.

In verse 9 Paul speaks of the fellowship of the mystery. Those who the Holy Spirit indwells make up the fellowship of believers, and that fellowship is the Church. There is the mystery of Christ and there is the mystery of the Church. The mystery of the Church is presented in another chapter. The mystery of Christ is now presented.

So, what was and what was not a mystery of Christ?

II. Christ the Messiah Was Not Hidden from the Sons of Men. Isaiah prophesied the coming of God in the flesh: "For unto us a child is born, unto us a son is given, and the government shall be upon his shoulder; and his name shall be called Wonderful, Counselor, The Mighty God, The Everlasting Father, The Prince of Peace" (Isa. 9:6). There is no ambiguity; God would come to this earth in the flesh as a child. Yet, He is the mighty God. The fulfillment of the prophecy was recorded in Luke 2:11: "For unto you is born this day in the city of David a Savior, who is Christ the Lord." Isaiah also prophesied of the one who would herald the coming of the king. "The voice of him that crieth in the wilderness, Prepare ye the way of the Lord, make straight in the desert a highway for our God" (Isa. 40:3). The fulfillment of the prophecy was recorded in Luke 3:2–4. John, the son of Zacharias, was the Lord's herald: "And he came into all the country about the Jordan, preaching the baptism of repentance for the remission of sins; As it is written in the book of the words of Isaiah, the prophet, saying, The voice of one crying in the wilderness, Prepare ye the way of the Lord, make his paths straight" (vv. 3–4).

Not only was the birth and ministry of Jesus prophesied to the Old Testament saints, the suffering of Jesus Christ, the Mighty God, was also prophesied. Isaiah prophesied of the suffering servant in Isaiah 50:6–7: "I gave my back to the smiters, and my cheeks to them that plucked off the hair; I hid not my face from shame and spitting. For the Lord God will help me; therefore shall I not be confounded; therefore have I set my face like a flint, and I know that I shall not be ashamed." Isaiah described the Lord's appearance as being so marred it was astounding (Isa. 2:14). Matthew and John record the fulfillment of Isaiah's prophecy in Matthew 26:67 and John 19:1 as Jesus was spit on before the Sanhedrin and Pilate had Jesus scourged and tortured. The prophecy by Zechariah concerning the suffering of Jesus is yet to be fulfilled when the Jews will realize what really took place at the cross. The Messiah was brutally beaten, humiliated, and crucified for the sins of the world. In Zechariah 12:10, the realization is profound: "And I will pour upon the house of David, and upon the inhabitants of Jerusalem, the Spirit of grace and of supplications; and they shall look upon me whom they have pierced, and they shall mourn for him, as one mourneth for his only son, and shall be in bitterness for him, as one that is in bitterness for his firstborn."

Yes, the rejection and crucifixion of Jesus was revealed to the Old Testament saints over 700 years before it took place. In Isaiah 53, the prophecy was given that Jesus would be despised and rejected of men; Jesus would be bruised for our iniquities, brought as a lamb to the slaughter, and his soul made an offering for sin. Through the sacrifice of Jesus Christ on the cross, He would justify many. Daniel prophesied that Messiah would be cut off in Daniel 9:26. The prophecy of Isaiah and Daniel comes to completion as recorded in the gospels. As Jesus was dying on the cross, He said, "It is finished" (John 19:30).

Jesus paid our sin debt, but thank God, it did not end there. As the women sought to anoint the body of Jesus and approached the tomb where Jesus had been buried, "the angel answered and said unto the women, Fear not; for I know that ye seek Jesus, who was crucified. He is not here; for he is risen as he said. Come, see the place where the Lord lay." Finally, the resurrection of Messiah would not have been hidden from the Old Testament saints. The psalmist said in Psalm 16:10: "For thou wilt not leave my soul in Sheol, neither wilt thou permit thine Holy One to see corruption." Messiah was not hidden from either Old or New Testament saints.

III. Differences between Old Testament and New Testament Saints: The coming of the Messiah would totally change the worship and privileges of the believer:

1. Animal sacrifices as sin offerings would cease. Once a year, the Levitical system required an animal sacrifice for the high priest for his sins and then a sacrifice for the whole congregation to be conducted by the high priest. This was called the Day of Atonement (Lev. 16). For individuals (priest, king, commoner) who confessed their sins during the rest of the year, an animal sacrifice was required and conducted by a priest (Lev. 4, 6). All this changed with the coming of the Lord Jesus Christ, the Messiah (Hebrews 9). "Neither by the blood of goats and calves, but by his own blood he entered in once into the holy place having obtained eternal redemption for us" (Heb. 9:12). "By which will we are sanctified through the offering of the body of Jesus Christ once for all" (Heb. 10:10).

2. No longer is any priest placed between man and God as it was for the Old Testament saint. Jesus removed the earthly priest of the Levitical system.

"Seeing, then, that we have a great high priest, that is passed into the heavens, Jesus, the Son of God, let us hold fast out profession. For we have not an high priest who cannot be touched with the feeling of our infirmities but was in all points tempted like as we are, yet without sin. Let us, therefore come boldly unto the throne of grace, that we may obtain mercy and find grace to help in time of need." (Heb. 4:14–15).

The New Testament believer can come boldly before the throne of God because of what Jesus has done.

3. The Old Testament saint at death went to Paradise or Abraham's bosom as indicated by Samuel coming back to speak to Saul when Saul visited the witch at Endor and when Lazarus died and was carried by the angels into the bosom of Abraham (1 Sam. 28:11–15; Luke 16: 22–23). The New Testament saint goes immediately to be with the Lord. "We are confident, I say, and willing rather to be absent for the body, and to be present with the Lord" (2 Cor. 5:8). The diagram below gives the scriptural context of what happened to a person at death in Old Testament times: Paradise, Sheol, Hades, and Gehenna.

Paradise – Sheol – Hades - Gehenna: What happens at Death?

Paradise	Sheol	Hades = Hell	Gehenna
· State of bliss and joy for the believer	· The grave	· Intermediate state of torment	· Lake of fire
· The destiny and experience of the redeemed.	1. Gen. 37:35; 42:38 The place of the good	1. Matt. 11:23 2. Matt. 16:18 3. Luke 16:23	1. Rev. 19:20 2. Matt. 5:22 3. Matt. 5:29–30 4. Luke 12:5
· Luke 23:43 Thief on the cross	2. 1 Samuel 2:6 3. Job 14:13		
· Revelation 22:2, 14 A new paradise	· Opposite of heaven: 1. Ps. 9:17 2. Prov. 23:14 The place of the wicked		
Spiritually alive.	Either spiritually alive or dead	Spiritually dead	Eternal torment
Will go to heaven	Will go to either paradise or hell	Will be cast into the lake of fire	
At 1st Resurrection		After 2nd Resurrection	Forever!

4. Old Testament saints are not the bride of Christ. Only the Church will be the bride of Christ. John the Baptist was the last Old Testament prophet and was beheaded before Christ spoke to Peter concerning establishing His Church. John was not a part of the Church. John the Baptist was the friend of the Bridegroom (John 3:39). The marriage of the Lamb, the Lord Jesus, to His bride, the Church, is recorded in Revelation 19:7–9. Those that are called to the marriage supper of the

Lamb are the Old Testament saints. "And he saith unto me, Write Blessed are they who are called unto the marriage supper of the Lamb and he saith unto me, These are true sayings of God" (Rev. 19:9).

5. The greatest difference between the Old and New Testament saints was Christ in you the hope of glory (Col. 1:27). As Paul spoke of the Church ("of the afflictions of Christ in my flesh for His body's sake *which is the church*" (Col. 1:24), Paul also spoke of:

> "Even the mystery which hath been hidden from ages and from generations, but now is made manifest to his saints, To whom God would make known what is the riches of the glory of *this mystery among the Gentiles, which is Christ in you the hope of glory*; Whom we preach, warning every man and teaching every man in all wisdom, that we may present everyman perfect in Christ Jesus." (Col. 1:26–28)

The promise of a light for the Gentiles, "To open the blind eyes to bring out the prisoners from the prison, and those who sit in darkness out of the prison house" had already been given (Isa. 42:6–7). That promise was reemphasized in Isaiah 49:6: "I will also give for a light to the Gentiles that thou mayest be my salvation unto the end of the earth." Both promises were in reference to Jesus Christ the suffering servant. The light shined, and the mystery was revealed at Calvary when Jesus was crucified for the sins of the world, for both Jew and Gentile. So how, after the crucifixion, was Christ in both believing Jew and Gentile?

IV. Christ In You the Hope of Glory Was Hidden: Christ indwelling the individual believer during the church age was the mystery. Christ indwells the believer; the church does not indwell the believer. In fact, the New Testament saint is part of the Church, the body of Christ. The believers do not indwell themselves. In Paul's letter to the Philippians, he said:

"For I know that this shall turn to my salvation through your prayer, and the supply of the Spirit of Jesus Christ, According to my earnest expectation and my hope that in nothing I shall be ashamed, but that with all boldness, as always, so now also Christ shall be magnified in my body, whether it be by life or by death. For to me to live is Christ and to die is gain." (Phil. 1:19–21)

The Spirit of Jesus Christ indwelled Paul, giving him the power to face death.

The Spirit of Jesus Christ and the Holy Spirit are one and the same. There is no difference. When Jesus told His disciples; "Nevertheless, I tell you the truth: It is expedient for you that I go away; for if I go not away, the Comforter will not come unto you; but if I depart, I will send him unto you" (John 16:7). The Comforter is the Holy Spirit. Again, Jesus told His disciples what the Spirit of Jesus Christ, the Comforter, the Spirit of truth would do: "Nevertheless, when he, the Spirit of truth, is come, he will guide you into all truth; for he shall not speak of himself, but whatever he shall hear, that shall he speak; and he will show you things to come. He shall glorify me; for he shall receive of mine, and shall show it unto you." (John 16:13–14). Jesus had told the disciples not only that He would send the Spirit of truth, but that the Spirit of truth would dwell in them. "Even the Spirit of truth whom the world cannot receive, because it seeth him not, neither knoweth him: but ye know him for he dwelleth with you, and shall be in you" (John 14:17).

In Old Testament times, the Holy Spirit came upon whom He may. The Holy Spirit did not indwell all individual believers as in the Church age. The Holy Spirit came upon Samson (Judg. 15:14), Saul (1 Sam. 10:6), Ezekiel (Ezek. 2:2), as well as other Old Testament saints but not all believers of that dispensation.

The first great outpouring of the Holy Spirit was at Pentecost. The mystery of Christ was that He indwelt believers at Pentecost, and He indwells every believer of the Church Age by His Spirit. Paul again emphasized the Godhead incarnate, Christ Jesus, when writing to the Colossians. Paul's desire for the Colossians and the believers at Laodicea was "that their hearts might be comforted, being knit together in love and unto all riches of the full assurance of understanding to the acknowledgement of the mystery of God and of the Father, and of Christ, In whom are hidden all the treasures of wisdom and knowledge" (Col. 2:2–3). By the indwelling Spirit of Christ (the Holy Spirit), the mystery of God is unlocked for the believer. The mystery of God is Christ, as incarnating the fulness of the Godhead, and provides all the divine wisdom and knowledge for the redemption and reconciliation of man. The treasure to be revealed of this wisdom and knowledge was what Jesus spoke of when He told the disciples He would send the Comforter. When the Comforter came, He would be "Christ in you the hope of glory." This is the *mystery of Christ*.

Chapter 2

The Mystery of Israel's Blindness

Romans 11:25

I. **Context:**

   ➢ Israel's spiritual blindness.
   ➢ The Gentile's spiritual blessing.

II. **A Remnant of Israel Saved in Paul's Day and during the Church Age (Rom. 11:1–6)**

   ➢ Israel is not cast away from God (v. 1).

   1. Witness and example 1: Paul himself, a Jew from the tribe of Benjamin.
   2. Witness and example 2: ElijahWhat he thought and what God revealed to Elijah; 7,000 reserved and protected.

   ➢ God's foreknowledge and election of a remnant: election according to grace.

   1. Remnants reserved.
   2. The election of Abraham.
   3. The election of a remnant of Jews to share the Gospel to the Gentiles.

III. Reasons for Israel's Blindness: (Rom. 11:7–10)

- ➤ Some elected as Paul, yet most blind to the grace of God.
- ➤ Blind due to idolatry as pointed out by the Old Testament prophets.
- ➤ Blind due to self-justification and legalism.

IV. Israel, the nation, is now blind and deaf to the Gospel (Rom. 11:8–10)

- ➤ A spirit of slumber even now.
- ➤ Their table has been a snare and a trap. A look back in history, Israel bowed down to other nations.

V. How Has God Used the Stumbling and Fall of Israel for Good? (Rom. 11:11–15).

- ➤ Israel's fall resulted in salvation coming to the Gentiles that God may provoke them to jealousy (vv. 11–12).
- ➤ Israel's restoration will be a witness to the world: as the dead made alive (vv. 13–15; Ezek. 37:1–14).

VI. Paul's warning to the Gentiles (Romans 11:16–24)

- ➤ The root is faithful Abraham (Jer. 11:16, the olive tree). Abraham was the olive tree that God planted, but the branches Israel bore evil fruit.
- ➤ Israel's branches are natural, not grafted as the Gentiles.
- ➤ Gentiles are to be careful not to boast for the root is what bears the tree and branches (the Gentiles). Gentiles are not of the original tree.
- ➤ Unbelief severed the branches (the unbelieving Jewish nation).

➢ The Gentile should stand in faith and fear that they not be cut off.

➢ How much easier it will be for God to graft the Jewish nation back into the root.

VII. The Restoration of Israel (Rom. 11:25–32)

➢ God's mystery of Israel's restoration (v. 25). What is that mystery?

➢ This is the fullness of the Gentiles, *not* the time of the Gentiles (v. 25).

1. The times of the Gentiles began with the Babylonian captivity of Judah under Nebuchadnezzar (Dan. 2:34, 35, 44) and will end with the coming of the Lord Jesus in glory (Rev. 19:11, 21).
2. The fullness of the Gentiles is the calling of the Gentiles during the Church age. Starting at Pentecost and ending with the rapture. (Acts 15:13–18; Rev. 3:10).

➢ The nation of Israel will be saved (vv. 26–32).

1. God's everlasting covenant with Israel (Jer. 31:31–34).
2. Israel in the tribulation period and the millennial reign.

The Mystery of Israel's Blindness
Romans 11:25

I. Context: In the letter to the Church at Rome, Paul warns Gentiles not to be high-minded when it comes to their thought that God had cast away His people, Israel, and rather provided salvation by grace to only the Gentiles (Rom. 11:20). The Gentiles were neither a substitute nor a replacement for the nation of Israel. The Gentiles were compared to a wild olive tree grafted into a good olive tree. The illustration Paul used is totally contrary to the process of grafting. Normally, the limbs of a good tree are grafted into a wild tree, not limbs from a wild tree grafted into a good tree. Paul emphasizes that God had not abandoned His chosen people, but they were blinded because of unbelief. That blindness of Israel would not be indefinite but would continue until the fulness of the Gentiles has been brought in (Rom. 11:25).

The unbelief and blindness began many years before the crucifixion of Jesus and the establishment of His Church. Israel, constantly rebelled against God and sought self-justification through works, and when the kingdom of God was at hand as Jesus walked among them, they rejected the Messiah. Paul emphasizes the blindness of Israel is a mystery to be pondered and examined by the Gentile believer. Paul wrote "For I would not, brethren, that ye should be ignorant of the mystery, lest ye should be wise in your own conceits; that blindness in part is happened to Israel, until the fulness of the Gentiles be come in" (Rom. 11:25). Blindness because of unbelief and blindness until the fulness of the Gentiles came in set the stage for hundreds of years of persecution and attempted annihilation of the Jews. However, Paul points out that God will again graft Israel into His goodness when they abide not still in unbelief (Rom. 11:23). When God grafts the natural branch of Israel back into the good tree, all Israel will be saved (Rom. 11:26). When the fulness of the Gentiles will come in, and when and how all Israel will be saved is the mystery.

II. A Remnant of Israel Saved during Paul's Day and during the Church Age (Rom. 11:1–6). Paul points out to the believers at Rome that he was one of those Israelites who was once blind to God's grace but had been saved by God's grace. It is interesting that the Holy Spirit led Paul to use the illustration of the blindness of Israel, as Paul was blinded on his way to Damascus by the Lord Jesus so that he might see the grace of God. Blinded that you might see is as contrary as a wild olive limb grafted into a good olive tree.

Not only did Paul use his own experience to illustrate God had not abandoned the nation of Israel, he also used the circumstance of Elijah at Mount Horeb. Elijah had slain the prophets of Baal at Mount Carmel and fled from Jezebel who swore to kill him. As Elijah reached Mount Horeb and was lodged in a cave, hiding from the army of Ahab, God in a still, small voice asked Elijah what he was doing there. Elijah replied to God, saying: "I have been very jealous of the LORD God of hosts: because the children of Israel have forsaken thy covenant, thrown down thine alters, and slain thy prophets with the sword; and I, even I only, am left; and they seek my life, to take it away." (1 Kings 19:14). God showed Elijah he was not alone: "Yet I have left me seven thousand in Israel, all the knees which have not bowed unto Baal, and every mouth hath not kissed him." (1 Kings 19:18). God showed Elijah that He had reserved a remnant of Israel then, and God had showed Paul He would continue to reserve a remnant of Israel according to the election of grace (Rom. 11:6).

God reserved a remnant in the person of Daniel, Ezekiel, Esther, and Mordecai during the seventy years of captivity of Israel under the Babylonians and Persians. At the end of the captivity, a remnant under the leadership of Ezra and Nehemiah was instrumental in rebuilding the temple and leading the people in obedience to God. As Jesus came into this world to die for the sins of mankind, John the Baptist, Simeon, and Anna all looked for redemption made possible by the Lord Jesus Christ. Finally, Paul states; "Even so then at this present time also there is a remnant according to the election of grace" (Rom. 11:5). Election and grace then, election and grace now, and election and grace in the future.

In Romans 11:2, Paul says "God hath not cast away his people which he foreknew and in verse 5, he says, "Even so then at this present time also there is a remnant according to the election of grace." The chapter entitled "The Mystery of God's Will" referenced Ephesians 1:3–14, the study of which focused on the sovereignty of God and the free will of man. Two words used to help describe the sovereignty of God is election and foreknowledge. Again, these two words are used by Paul to describe God's special relationship with the nation of Israel:

1. **Election:** the Greek word for election is *ekloge* (ἐκλογή) denotes a picking out, selection, that which is chosen.[4] In 1 Peter 1:2, Peter is speaking to the elect according to the *foreknowledge of God.* "Elect according to the foreknowledge of God, the Father, through sanctification of the Spirit, unto obedience and sprinkling of the blood of Jesus Christ: Grace unto you and peace, be multiplied."

2. **Foreknowledge:** the Greek word for foreknowledge is *proginosko* (προγινώσκ▢)to know before used of divine knowledge. Also, the Greek word *prognosis* (**πρόγνωσις**) is an aspect of omniscience implied in God's warnings, promises, and predictions.[5] Acts 15:18 states: "Known unto God are all his works from the beginning of the world." In Romans 8:29, *foreknowledge is the prerequisite to predestinate:* "For whom he did foreknow he also did predestinate to be conformed to the image of his Son, that he might be the firstborn among many brethren."

---

[4]   W.E. Vine, *An Expository Dictionary of New Testament Words.*

[5]   Ibid.

A review of the context of the two words show God elected Israel through His foreknowledge. That election was made plain when God covenanted with Abram:

> Now the LORD had said unto Abram, Get thee out of thy country, and from thy kindred, and from thy father's house, unto a land that I will shew thee: And I will make of thee a great nation, and I will bless thee, and make thy name great; and thou shalt be a blessing: And I will bless them that bless thee, and curse him that curseth thee: and in thee shall all families of the earth be blessed." (Gen. 12:1–3)

God has for thousands of years blessed the nations that blessed the people of Israel and cursed the nations that cursed Israel. God has blessed all nations by providing salvation by grace through faith in the Lord Jesus Christ. The bridge between God's election of Abraham and the Gentile world is that remnant of Jews that God elected and protected was used to deliver the Gospel of Christ.

III. *Reasons for Israel's Blindness* (Rom. 11:7–10): God has never reneged on His promise to Abraham. However, God did set forth conditions of obedience to Israel when He gave them the law through Moses. God's message to the Israelites at Sinai was: "Now therefore, if ye will obey my voice indeed, and keep my covenant, then ye shall be a peculiar treasure unto me above all people for all the earth is mine: And ye shall be unto me a kingdom of priests and an holy nation. These are the words which thou shalt speak unto the children of Israel" (Exod. 19:4–5). The promise to Abraham was not conditional, but blessings based on obedience to the law were conditional, and Israel failed miserably as all of mankind fails to meet God's law. The misinterpretation of the purpose of the Law and the pursuit of self-justification by works negated Israel from becoming a kingdom of priests and a holy nation.

The Law was intended by God to be a schoolmaster to bring us to Christ so that we might be justified by faith (Gal. 3:23), not by the works of the law. Paul poses the question in Romans 11:7, "What then? Israel hath not obtained that which he seeketh for; but the election hath obtained it, and the rest were blinded." What Israel attempted could not reconcile them to God. First, their choice of idolatry blinded them to the grace of God. They chose to worship many gods as a substitute for the God of creation. This played out throughout the Old Testament. Second, self-justification blinded them to the grace of God as Jesus came to seek and save that which was lost. The results of their pursuit of idolatry and self-righteousness yielded chastisement by God for centuries.

Their blindness due to idolatry was addressed many times by the Old Testament prophets. God warned Israel time and time again of their idolatry and iniquity. The prophet Amos, who prophesied in the northern kingdom, warned both the northern and southern kingdom of God's judgment; "Hear this word that the LORD hath spoken against you, O children of Israel, against the whole family which I brought up from the land of Egypt, saying, You only have I known of all the families of the earth: therefore I will punish you for all your iniquities" (Amos 3:1–2). As Isaiah warned Judah and Jerusalem of the impending invasion by Babylon and their failure to grasp the discipline of God, he said they would be as people in a deep sleep; "For the Lord hath poured out upon you the spirit of deep sleep and hath closed your eyes: the prophets and your rulers, the seers hath he covered." (Isa. 29:10). Isaiah depicted Judah's leadership as blind, ignorant, dumb dogs: "His watchmen are blind: they are all ignorant, they are all dumb dogs, they cannot bark; sleeping, lying down, loving to slumber" (Isa. 56:10). Jeremiah painted a bleak picture of the religious leadership of the southern kingdom: "The Priests said not, Where is the LORD? And they that handle the law knew me not: the pastors also transgressed against me, and the prophets prophesied by Baal, and walked after things that do not profit" (Jer. 2:8). Zephaniah who was a prophet in the time of Jeremiah warned of the coming judgment of Judah; "A Day of the trumpet and alarm against the fenced cities, and against the high towers. And I will bring distress upon men, that they shall walk like blind men, because they have sinned against the LORD: and their blood shall be poured out as dust and their flesh as the dung" (Zeph. 1:17).

God judged the northern kingdom by using Assyria to carry them into captivity. (2 Kings 17:6). The blindness of their idolatry was recorded in 2 Kings 17

> "And walked in the statues of the heathen whom the LORD cast out from before the children of Israel, and of the kings of Israel which they had made. And the children of Israel did secretly those things that were not right against the LORD their God, and they built them high places in all their cities, from the tower of the watchmen to the fenced city. And they set them up images and groves in every high hill, and under every green tree: and there they burnt incense in all the high places, as did the heathen whom the LORD carried away before them; and wrought wicked things to provoke the LORD to anger; For they served idols, whereof the Lord had said unto them, Ye shall not do this thing. Yet the Lord testified against Israel, and against Judah, by all the prophets and by all the seers, saying, Turn ye from your evil ways and keep my commandments and my statues, according to all the law which I commanded your fathers, and which I sent to you by my

servants the prophets. Notwithstanding they would not hear, but hardened their necks, like to the neck of their fathers, that did not believe in the LORD their God. "(2 Kings 17:8–14)

God judged the southern kingdom by using Babylon to carry them into captivity. The southern kingdom was removed in two deportations by King Nebuchadnezzar and carried away to Babylon (2 Kings 24:11–25:10). The poster child of evil was King Manasseh of Judah who made his sons pass through the fire, observed times and enchantments, dealt with familiar spirits and wizards, built up again the high places and the altars for Baal, worshiped the host of heaven, and did more evil than the nations that God cast out before Israel (2 Kings 21:1–9). Although Manasseh eventually humbled himself before the LORD and knew that the LORD was God (2 Chron. 33:11–13), the LORD did not turn from the fierceness of his great wrath, with which his anger was kindled against Judah because of all the provocations with which Manasseh had provoked Him (2 Kings 23:25–26).

Not only was all Israel, with the exception of a remnant, blind during the Old Testament as they went a whoring after other gods (Hos. 9:1), they were blind when Jesus walked among them. When the Jews came out of captivity, they exchanged their walk after other gods for adherence to the law and tradition of the elders as the way of salvation. They embraced pure legalism as their justification before God. The exchange was made manifest when the scribes and Pharisees came to Jesus and asked, "Why do thy disciples transgress the tradition of the elders? For they wash not their hands when they eat bread. But he answered and said unto them, Why do ye also transgress the commandment of God by your tradition?" (Matt. 15:2–3). The tradition allowed the Jews to avoid taking care of their parents by claiming what they had would be a gift to God, ignoring the commandment to honor father and mother. Jesus went on to tell the religious leaders;

"Ye hypocrites, well did Esaias prophesy of your saying, This people draweth nigh unto me with their mouth, and honoreth me with their lips; but their heart is far from me. But in vain they do worship me, teaching for doctrines the commandments of men" (Matt. 15:7–9). John shows the Jew's attitude toward Jesus was the fulfillment of the prophecy of Isaiah in John 12:37–40, when John wrote:

> "But though he had done so many miracles before them, yet they believed not on him: That the saying of Esaias the prophet might be fulfilled, which he spake, Lord, who hath believed our report? And to whom hath the arm of the Lord been revealed? Therefore they could not believe, because that Esaias said again, He hath blinded their eyes, and hardened their heart that they should not see with their eyes, nor understand with their heart, and be converted, and I should heal them."

The Pharisees exercised many other acts of legalism against Jesus for healing on the Sabbath, allowing a woman who was a sinner to touch him, and eating with tax collectors and sinners as defined by the religious leaders.

IV. Israel the Nation Is Now Blind and Deaf to the Gospel (Rom. 11:8–10): The prophets as well as Jesus depicted Israel as blind, ignorant, dumb, legalistic, self-righteous, hard-hearted, and entitled. In fact, the last Old Testament prophet, John the Baptist, called the Pharisees and Sadducees a generation of vipers and told them, "And think not to say within yourselves, We have Abraham to our father: for I say unto you, that God is able of these stones to raise up children unto Abraham" (Matt. 3:9). Also, as Jesus pronounced woe upon the Pharisees, calling them hypocrites, blind guides, fools, and blind serpents and a generation of vipers (Matt. 23:13–36). Paul emphasized in Rom.11:8 the total depravity of his people by referencing Isaiah 29:10, that God had given Israel the spirit of slumber with blind eyes and deaf ears.

Paul, then in Romans 11:9, references Psalm 69:22–23, a Psalm of David, saying: "Let their table be made a snare, and a trap, and a stumbling block, and a recompence unto them: Let their eyes be darkened, that they may not see, and bow down their back always." History shows that has been the plight of the Jews for centuries. Looking back on the history of the persecution of the Jews, snares and traps and stumbling blocks have perpetually been cast before them in persecution as they have been forced to bow down to other nations. Here is a backward look: [6,7,8]

1. Currently, no one can dispute that the tiny nation of Israel in 2021 is at the center of international controversy. Whether it is the United Nations opposition, the establishment of embassies in Jerusalem, territories claimed by the Palestinians and held by Israel, or the threatened policy of annihilation of the nation by Muslim nations, such as Iran. Even in the month of May 2021, hundreds of missiles were launched into Israel from Gaza by the Palestinian militants sponsored by Iran in a proxy attack. These types of attacks have been going on for decades.

2. After World War II, General Eisenhower made sure through careful documentation and filming that the atrocities committed against the Jews during the war (1945) were recorded. At the center of Adolf Hitler's policy was the extermination of the Jews. Although the Jews were not an armed force, it was

---

[6]   Joshua J. Mark, "Israel," Ancient History Encyclopedia.

[7]   P.E. Grosser, E.G. Halperin, *Anti-Semitism: Causes and Effects.*

[8]   The Embassy of Israel in South Africa, "History of Israel: Timeline."

the primary victim of the war with the murder of 6,000,000 Jews by the Third Reich.

3. In Europe, from AD 1290 to 1881, millions of Jews were either slaughtered or expelled from England, Germany, France, Poland, Lithuania, Portugal, Italy, Ukraine, and Russia. Europe has hated the Jews, and what has been cast upon this people was at the center of the policy of many of the nations of the world. The Jewish people have been fugitives wherever they have fled.

4. From AD 623 to 717, the Jews were persecuted and murdered by Muhammad and the Islamic caliphates. Islamic policy then and today is extermination of the Jews.

5. In AD 136, 580,000 Jews were killed when they revolted the third time against the Roman Empire.

6. In AD 70, the Jewish historian Josephus records the slaughter of 1,100,000 Jews, 97,000 taken captive and enslaved, and the total destruction of Jerusalem by the Romans. [9]

7. The Seleucid Empire, part of the Macedonian Empire established after the death of Alexander the Great, was a thorn in the side of the Jews. Antiochus IV Epiphanes, one of the Hellenistic kings (175–164 BC), was one who persecuted and taunted the Jews by profaning the temple at Jerusalem by offering pigs on the temple altar. His policy was the elimination of Jewish culture.

---

[9]   William Whiston, *The Works of Flavius Josephus, Book VI*, Chapter IX, p. 469.

8. From 167 BC to 37 BC, the nation was somewhat independent and was ruled by the Maccabees until 40 BC, when the land became a province of the Roman Empire. The independent identity as a nation state ceased under Roman policy.[10]

9. The Jewish people and their land were ping-ponged among nations as the empires of the Greeks under the leadership of Alexander the Great (356–323 BC), the Persians under the leadership of Cyrus the Great (599–529 BC) and the Babylonians under the leadership Nebuchadnezzar, king of Babylon (605–562 BC) conquered, persecuted, and dominated the Jewish people. As secular history points out these facts, even more important is the fact that the prophet Daniel prophesied of these nations and the events that would occur over this period from 605 BC until 40 BC.

10. Prior to the southern kingdom of Judah and Benjamin having been enslaved and carried off to Babylon, the southern kingdom was under the rule of twenty kings over a period of 347 years (933–586 BC). Only eight of these kings were deemed by the Bible to be godly kings. Although there were periods of revival, the remaining twelve kings became progressively more and more rebellious against the God of the Old Testament. Idolatry and wickedness reached its peak under King Manasseh. This wicked king built up the high places, made altars to Baal, worshiped and made altars for the host of heaven, sacrificed his sons in fire, observed times, used enchantments, dealt with mediums and wizards, and set up carved images in the temple. God proclaimed through the prophets in 2 Kings 21:9–13:

---

[10]   The Maccabees/Hasmoneans: History & Overview, https://www.jewishvirtuallibrary.org.

"Manasseh seduced them to do more evil than did the nations whom the LORD destroyed before the children of Israel. And the LORD spoke by his servants, the prophets, saying, Because Manasseh, king of Judah, hath done these abominations, and hath done wickedly above all that the Amorites, did who were before him and hath made Judah also to sin with his idols; Therefore, thus saith the LORD God of Israel, Behold, I am bringing such evil upon Jerusalem and Judah that whosoever heareth of it, both of his ears shall tingle, And I will stretch over Jerusalem the line of Samaria, and the plummet of the house of Ahab; and I will wipe Jerusalem as a man wipeth a dish, wiping it, and turning it upside down."

As the rebellion simmered, the kingdom was constantly in fear of being eliminated. The temple in Jerusalem was destroyed by the Babylonians in 598 BC and the aristocracy, scribes, and craftsmen deported to Babylon. After further rebellion against Babylon, military campaigns from 589–582 BC destroyed Jerusalem. The southern kingdom of Judah ceased when Nebuchadnezzar killed King Zedekiah's sons and put out the eyes of Zedekiah and took him back to Babylon, imprisoning him until the day of his death (Jer. 52:5–15).

11. Prior to the northern kingdom of Israel (the other ten tribes) being enslaved and the population relocated by the Assyrian King Sargon II in 722 BC, the kingdom was ruled by nineteen wicked kings for 212 years (933–721 BC). The kingdom was initiated when, after Solomon's death and his son Rehoboam ascended to the throne, Jeroboam the son of Nebat led the ten tribes to split the kingdom (1 Kings 12). Idolatry was Jeroboam's first order to consolidate the ten tribes as one nation, separate from Judah, by making two calves of gold, saying to Israel,

"Behold, O Israel, thy gods" (1 Kings 12:28). This was done to keep the ten tribes from going to Jerusalem to worship, thus risking a reconsolidation. For this idolatry, God removed the northern kingdom whose capital was Samaria (2 Kings 17)

12. Although there was civil war between the house of Saul and the House of David, and within the house of David, the consolidated kingdom of all tribes of Israel under the Kings Saul, David, and Solomon, were known as the golden age of unity (1080–970 BC). A true united kingdom was achieved under King David. Under David and Solomon, the united Israel was respected if not feared by the surrounding nations. First Kings 10:23–24 records: "So King Solomon exceeded all the kings of the earth in riches and wisdom. And all the earth consulted Solomon, to hear his wisdom which God had put in his heart." Israel in that day influenced the foreign policy of all known nations. Obedience to God resulted in blessings for Israel.

13. After much of the land of Canaan was conquered by Israel and the great military leader Joshua died, the judges of Israel (1400–1050 BC) settled disputes among the tribes. Israel was made up of loose-knit tribes with their own agenda. Their agenda was driven by a new evil generation. Judges 2:10–11 states: "and there arose another generation after them who knew not the LORD, nor yet the works which he had done for Israel. And the children of Israel did evil in the sight of the LORD, and served Baalim." The Israelites were constantly persecuted by many of the people that surrounded them (Philistines, Canaanites, Sidonians, Hivites, Hittites, Amorites, Perizzites, king of Mesopotamia, king of Moab, Midianites, Ammonites). Their persecution was the direct result of disobedience toward God. The tribes would fall deep into sin, repent, and God would raise up a judge to deliver them. They

would then fall back into sin and the cycle would be repeated. Idolatry resulted in God's discipline.

14. After forty years of wandering, Israel was purged of those who were rebellious against God's leadership. In Numbers 14:29–30, God tells Moses:

"Your carcasses shall fall in this wilderness; and all who were numbered of you, according to our whole number, from twenty years old and upward, who have murmured against me, Doubtless ye shall not come into the land, concerning which I swore to make you dwell therein, except Caleb, the son Jephunneh, and Joshua, the son of Nun."

After the wandering, a time of great military success occurred as a young nation struck fear in all of the land of Canaan. The city states in all of Canaan were all terrified. Joshua 1:9 records Rahab's observation of the fear of these city states: "And she said unto the men, I know that the LORD hath given you the land, and that your terror is fallen upon us, and that all the inhabitants of the land faint because of you." This great mass of people coming out of the desert who had already conquered those nations across the Jordan river were front and center to the policy of the nations inhabiting the land of Canaan.

15. Enslaved by the Egyptian (1450–1410 BC), Israel flourished as long as Joseph was remembered by the Egyptians. However, when the Egyptians forgot what Joseph did for Egypt, Israel was enslaved. Under enslavement, a nation was born and was then delivered according to God's purpose (Gen. 15:13–16).

When one reflects on these facts and realizes that over a period of 3,400 years, the Jewish people and the nation of Israel has been a major part of the policy of the world's dominant nations is mind boggling. How is that the Jewish people have been so prominent in world affairs for so long and have not melted into other societies as most nations are today? How is it that the people have been so hated by so many, yet they continue until today? How is it that a nation ceases to exist (Babylonian captivity, Roman dominance), with its people and culture intact? Well, it is because God has a purpose for his chosen people that began with His covenant with Abram and He will bring it to fruition.

V. How Has God Used the Stumbling and Fall of Israel for Good? *(Rom. 11:11–15).* When God promised Abraham, He would make of Abraham a great nation and through him all the families of the earth would be blessed, God reinforced His promise over and over (Gen. 12:2–3; 18:18; 22:18; 26:4; 28:14). Israel was chosen by God to be a holy people unto the LORD. They were chosen to be a special people above all people on the earth. Israel was not chosen because of anything they could offer but because God loved them and because He would keep the oath which He had sworn to Abraham, Isaac, and Jacob (Deut. 7:6–8). God's promise and purpose would be established for Abraham. However, God's will for Israel to become a kingdom of priests would not be accomplished (Exod. 19:6). Israel would become the people through which Jesus Christ the Messiah would come (Matt. 1:1–17), but they would reject Jesus and crucify him. Israel failed as a priesthood people, but God's promise that all families would be blessed through Abraham did not fail. Salvation came to the Gentiles.

Israel's fall, though catastrophic, was not terminal and will not remain indefinitely. Israel will again stand up as dry bones that are covered with sinew and flesh and made alive. In verse 15, Paul poses the question: "What shall the receiving of them be, but life from the dead." The reference is probably to the vision of the valley of dry bones in Ezekiel 37:1–14. Ezekiel was shown a valley of dry bones and commanded to prophesy to the bones to hear the word of the Lord. The bones came together with sinews, flesh, and skin. Ezekiel was then told to prophesy to the wind that breath would enter into the bodies, and as he did a great army stood up. Ezekiel was then told that those standing was the whole house of Israel that God would put His Spirit in them that they might live. Israel will be quickened from spiritual death to spiritual life. When will Israel's spiritual restoration take place here lies the mystery.

V. *Paul's Warning to the Gentiles* (Rom. 11:16–24): In the meantime, how should Gentiles view what God has revealed by Paul? Paul warns the Gentiles to not be high-minded but to fear God. For if God would chasten the apple of His eye would God not also judge the Gentiles' pride, arrogance, and unbelief (Deut. 32:10; Zech. 2:8)? Israel was the green olive tree that was rooted in God's promise to Abraham. Jeremiah gives the context:

> "The Lord called thy name, A green olive tree, fair, and of goodly fruit with noise of a great tumult he hath kindled fire upon it, and the branches of it are broken. For the LORD of hosts, that planted thee, hath pronounced evil against them, for the evil of the house of Israel and of the house of Judah, which they have done against themselves to provoke me to anger in offering incense unto Baal."

God planted the olive tree, and faithful, believing Abraham was the established root. The olive tree's limbs had produced evil fruit, and God broke the limbs and burned them. Contrary to nature, God then grafted wild olive limbs (Gentiles) into the good tree and root. The Gentiles are required to produce good fruit or else they too would be severed. Jesus pointed this out to his disciples when He said: "I am the vine, ye are the branches: He that abideth in me, and I in him, the same bringeth forth much fruit for without me ye can do nothing" (John 15:5).

Paul lays the foundation for Israel's blindness to be changed to great insight when he says it will be much easier for Israel to be grafted back into the original olive tree from which they were severed. In fact, Paul was a great example of the process. Paul, as many Jews today, was well schooled in the Old Testament, and when his eyes were opened to the truth of the gospel, he was able to see and apply God's Word immediately and very clearly. Paul had a PhD in Old Testament Law, and when he surrendered to Jesus, he burst forth with much fruit, the fruit of the Spirit. When the fulness of the Gentiles has come in, so will all of Israel be grafted back and produce good fruit. How and when Israel will be grafted back will complete the mystery.

VII. The Restoration of Israel (Rom. 11:25–32): The key to knowing the beginning of the restoration of Israel is to determine what is meant by "the fullness of the Gentiles be come in. Paul said in verse 25, "For I would not, brethren that ye should be ignorant of this mystery, lest ye should be wise in your own conceits: that blindness in part is happened to Israel, until the fullness of the Gentiles be come in." A distinction must be made between the fullness of the Gentiles and the time of the Gentiles. The fullness of the Gentiles is the Church age that begin at Pentecost and will end with the rapture of the Church. Paul expounds on this time period in Ephesians 4:12–13 when he speaks of the spiritual gifts that were given to the Church: "For the perfection of the saints for the work of the ministry for the edifying of the body of Christ, Till we all come in the unity of the faith, and of the knowledge of the Son of God, unto a perfect man, unto the measure of the stature of the fullness of Christ;" The fullness of the Gentiles refers to the number of people who are saved during the Church age. When the last person is saved during the Church age, the fullness will be complete and the Church will be raptured. (See the chapter on the "Mystery of the Resurrection").

The time of the Gentiles is characterized in Luke 21:24, "And they shall fall by the edge of the sword, and shall be led away captive into all nations; and Jerusalem shall be trodden down by the Gentiles, until the times of the Gentiles be fulfilled." The times of the Gentiles refers to the period of time that began with the conquering of Jerusalem and the destruction of the temple by Nebuchadnezzar and the Babylonians in 586 BC. The end of the times of the Gentiles will come with the second coming of Jesus Christ the Messiah. It is called times because Israel has been dominated by Gentile powers, including Babylon, Persia, Greece, Rome, and other Gentile nations for centuries.

With the fullness of the Gentiles complete and the Church raptured, God will redeem His chosen people. Paul said in Romans 11:26–27, "And so all Israel shall be saved; as it is written, There shall come out of Zion the Deliverer, and shall turn away ungodliness from Jacob; For this is my covenant unto them, when I shall take away their sins." How will God orchestrate His great redemption of the Jews? When the tribulation begins with the seal judgments opened by Jesus Christ, the sixth seal will open and show the heaven depart as a scroll, rolled together revealing Jesus sitting on his throne to those on earth. Most people of the earth will hide from Jesus and hope for death (Rev. 6:12–17). Others, including many Jews, will see Jesus as He really is and respond as Zechariah prophesied, "And I will pour upon the house of David, and upon the inhabitants of Jerusalem, the Spirit of grace and of supplications; and they shall look upon me whom they have pierced, and they shall mourn for him, as one mourneth for his only son and shall be in bitterness for him, as one that is in bitterness for his first-born." As the seal judgments are being poured out, God will raise up 144,000 Jews to preach the gospel of the kingdom (Matt. 24:14), and many Gentiles and Jews will be saved (Rev. 7:9; 15:1–3).

As the Spirit of grace is poured out, the Jewish people will "get it.' They will realize finally what has been going on all along. They will place in context and believe what Jeremiah said in Jeremiah 31:31–34:

> "Behold the days come, saith the LORD, that I will make a new covenant with house of Israel, and with house of Judah, Not according to the covenant that I made with their fathers in the day that I took them by the hand to bring them out of the land of Egypt, which, my covenant, they broke, although I was an husband unto them, saith the LORD; But this shall be the covenant that I will make with the house of Israel: After those days, saith the LORD, I will put my law in their inwards parts, and write it in their hearts, and will be their God, and they shall be my people. And they shall teach no more everyman his neighbor, and every man his brother, saying, Know the LORD; *for they shall all know me*, from the least of them unto the greatest of them, saith the LORD for I will forgive their iniquity, and I will remember Their sins no more."

They will turn to Jesus with the zeal of Paul. Persecution and death will not deter them. The whole nation will turn to Jesus their Messiah of whom they will only then recognize.

The believing Jews who survive the tribulation and go into the millennial reign will respond as Zechariah prophesied, will know Jesus as Jeremiah prophesied, and be saved as Paul was led to write that all Israel shall be saved (Rom. 11:25). The blindness of Israel to the Gospel is real today and has been for centuries. However, when the olive limb is grafted back into the olive tree, when the scales from their eyes are removed, they, too, will see and understand the mystery of their blindness and what Jesus did for His bride the Church during their blindness.

"Oh, the depth of the riches both of the wisdom and knowledge of God! How unsearchable are his judgements, and his ways past finding out!" (Rom. 11:33)

Chapter 3

The Mystery of the Church

The Church, a Hidden Mystery Not Shown to Other Ages

Ephesians 3:1–12; Colossians 1:24–27

I. Context:

- ➤ The mystery of the church was not revealed to either prophet or angel.
- ➤ Understand the mystery of Christ before studying the mystery of the church.

II. Jesus Christ and His Church Are Intertwined; They Cannot Be Separated:

- ➤ The Church is the Body of Christ (Col. 1:24).
- ➤ Christ is the head of the Church (Col. 1:18).
- ➤ The Church is made up of both Jew and Gentile (1 Cor. 12:12–13).
- ➤ The fellowship of the mystery is the Church (Eph. 3:9).

III. The Body of the Church Was Created and Confirmed by Jesus:

1. The Church announced by Jesus (Matt. 16:13–20).

2. The Church commissioned by Jesus (Matt. 28:19–20).
3. The Church established (Acts 1:8,21).
4. The Church equipped for service (Rom. 12; 1 Cor. 12).

IV. *None of God's Creation Saw the Church Coming into Existence.* *(Eph. 3:3–6, 9)*

➢ Principalities and powers in heavenly places did not know (Eph. 3:10).

1. Angels, both Good and fallen (evil) did not know.
2. Satan did not know.
3. Angels would learn from the church by looking into the work of the Holy Spirit in the church (1 Pet. 1:12).
4. Angels watch how the Christian behaves (1 Cor. 11:10).
5. The great host of Angels have a great interest in the believer as they guard and minister to the believer (Matt. 18:10; Heb. 1:14).

➢ Old Testament Prophets had no perception of the Church.

1. Isaiah and Ezekiel prophesied of the Messiah but not the church (Isa. 49–51; Ezek. 11–21).
2. Daniel saw the coming of great tribulation and the resurrection (Dan. 12:1–2) but not the church.
3. Daniel did not see the church (Dan. 12:12) as Jesus spoke to his apostles. (Matt. 24:21) about the same great tribulation.
4. The Old Testament prophets could not visualize the Church consisting of Jews and Gentiles as fellow heirs of the same body of Christ (Eph. 3:6).

➢ Prophets were silent from Malachi to Matthew.

V. The Church Shows the Manifold Wisdom of God (Eph. 3:10)

> ➤ Salvation for the nations was revealed but not the Church (Isa. 44:1; 49:6; Mal. 1:11).
> ➤ God revealed the Church through Jesus Christ as believers would be capable of understanding (John16:13).
> ➤ No congregation of Gentiles and Jews serving the Lord would exist if it were not for the church.

The Mystery of the Church
Ephesians 3:1–12; Colossians 1:24–27

I. Context: The mystery of the Church was not revealed to either the Old Testament prophets or the angels, either good or bad. The body of Christ composed of both Jews and Gentiles in one fellowship was not revealed. This is the mystery. Already, the mystery of Christ has been introduced in the previous chapter. Where the mystery of Christ was not made known to the sons of men, the mystery of the Church was hidden from both man and angel (Eph. 3:9–10). One must study the mystery of Christ in order to understand the mystery of the Church.

II. Jesus Christ and His Church are Intertwined; They Cannot be Separated. The church is the body of Christ, and Jesus is the head of the church (Col. 1:18–24}. In Ephesians 3:9, Paul speaks of the fellowship of the mystery: "And to make all men see what is the *fellowship of the mystery* which from the beginning of the ages hath been hidden in God, who created all things by Jesus Christ. To the intent that now, unto the *principalities and powers in heavenly places*, might be known by the church the manifold wisdom of God." What makes up the fellowship of the mystery? It is that body of believers, both Jew and Gentile, who are indwelled by the Spirit of Christ (the Holy Spirit). It is the Church (1 Cor. 12:12–14).

III. The Body of the Church Was Created and Confirmed by Jesus: The Church was announced, commissioned, established, and equipped by Jesus. In Matthew 16:13–20, Jesus asked his disciples: "Who do men say that I the Son of man am?" Peter replied "Thou art the Christ, the Son of the living God." Jesus then told Peter that flesh and blood did not reveal this to him but God the Father had revealed this truth to him. Then Jesus said, "That thou art Peter (Petros, a stone), and upon this rock (Petra, a massive rock), I will build my church, and the gates of hades shall not prevail against it." Jesus gave His great commission to His disciples and the Church in Matthew 28:19–20: "Go ye, therefore, and teach all nations, baptizing them in the name of the Father, and of the Son, and of the Holy Spirit, Teaching them to observe all things whatsoever I have commanded you; and, lo, I am with you always, even unto the end of the age. Amen." The book of Acts provides the chronological history of the churches being established from Jerusalem to Asia Minor, to Greece and to Rome. In the three missionary journeys Paul conducted, many were won to Christ and joined the body of Christ, the church. The Holy Spirit (the Spirit of Christ, Phil. 1:19) equipped and confirmed these churches with spiritual gifts. The gifts were given to authenticate authority and enable the believer to carry out the Lord's great commission (Rom. 12; 1 Corinthians 12).

IV. None of God's Creation Saw the Church Coming into Existence. The angels and the principalities and powers in heavenly places already knew Christ. Christ was there at the creation of every angel, including Satan. The angels were there when Christ created the heavens and earth (Gen. 1:1; Col. 1:16, 3–9). The angels were there when Christ spoke to Abraham (Gen. 18) and when Christ spoke to Moses and Joshua (Exod. 3:1–6; Josh. 5:13–15). He was seen and worshiped in heaven by them. What the angels, good and evil, Satan included, did not see coming was the Church, the "fellowship of the mystery." The Church would display the manifold wisdom of God to the angels (Eph.

3:10). Satan must have stood in awe as the body of Christ, the Church, came into being and his defeat became inevitable.

All angels would learn much through the Church as they watched the believers; (1 Cor. 4:9; 11:10). The angels also have a desire to look into the things of the Church (1 Pet. 1:12). To understand the great mystery of the church the angels watch the believer, and they watch over the believer. Jesus warned those who would offend a new child of God: "Take heed that ye despise not one of these little ones; for I say unto you, That in heaven their angels do always behold the face of my Father which is in heaven" (Matt. 18:10). The angels are ministering spirits, sent forth to minister for them who shall be heirs of salvation (Heb. 1:14). It is by the church that the manifold wisdom of God is revealed to the spiritual world. It is by the Church that angels learn of the grace and love of the Lord Jesus Christ for His creation.

Not only was the coming of the church hidden from the heavenly host, it was hidden from the Old Testament prophets. Isaiah saw the coming of Messiah, the suffering servant, who was also given as a light to the Gentiles (nations), but he prophesied nothing of the church (Isa. 49–53). Isaiah's prophecy centered around the Jews. Daniel did not see the coming of the Church. Ezekiel prophesied of the Israel's idolatrous leaders, the resulting judgment, and the coming of Messiah but not the church (Ezek. 14–21). Daniel prophesied of the great tribulation (Dan. 12:1–2, 9–13), the same that Jesus spoke of in Matthew 24:21, but he did not speak of the Church. Daniel's questions to God were about Israel. He had no concept of the Church. In Daniel 12:9, God told Daniel, "Go thy way, Daniel; for the words are closed up and sealed till the time of the end." The Church, the body of Christ was not revealed and the end time regarding Israel was not revealed to Daniel. The revelation of the church was silent from Malachi to Matthew. The time of the Maccabees revealed nothing of the Church

(1 and 3 Maccabees, Catholic Bible). The church was first revealed by Jesus to the disciples (Matt. 16:18).

V. The Church Shows the Manifold Wisdom of God to All Who Will Trust Jesus as Lord and Savior. The Old Testament prophets knew salvation for the nations would come, but they were not shown how God would make that happen. Jesus revealed His plan and purpose for the Church as His disciples became equipped to understand. The full equipping would not happen until the Comforter, the Holy Spirit, would come. Great enlightenment came to believers as Jesus promised He would send the Comforter (the Holy Spirit) that would guide them into all truth and show them things to come (John 16:13). The plan and promise of the power of the Spirit of God toward the Church was put prominently on display at Pentecost. Many believed then and many mocked. Many mock today because it is a mystery the lost do not understand.

Chapter 4

The Mystery of Christ and the Church

Ephesians 5:32

I. *Context:*

- ➢ The position of the believer during the Church age.
- ➢ God's glory revealed through the marriage relationship.

II. *What the scripture says about the body of Christ:*

- ➢ The body (the Church) is made possible by Christ suffering for our sin (1 Pet. 3:18).
- ➢ The body is a spiritual union (Col. 2:13).
- ➢ The body consists of many members (1 Cor. 12:12–14).
- ➢ No member has either self-serving rights or authority (1 Cor. 6:19).
- ➢ What the believer as part of the body should understand as it relates to marriage.

III. *What the scripture says about the bride of Christ*

- ➢ Christ gave Himself for His bride, the Church (Eph. 5:25–27).
- ➢ Christ has prepared a great marriage ceremony for His bride (Rev. 19:7–9).

➤ Christ will clothe His bride with His righteousness (2 Cor. 5:21; Rev. 19:8).

➤ What the believer should understand as it relates to being part of the bride of Christ.

IV. The Mystery of Christ and the Church exemplified by Christian marriage (Eph. 5:21–33).

➤ How the wife in marriage exemplifies the Church as the bride of Christ.

1. Submission as unto the Lord (Eph. 5:22).
2. Unity and order in the marriage.

➤ How the husband in marriage exemplifies Christ with:

1. Unbounded love.
2. Willful love (Luke 22:42).
3. Purposed commitment (Eph. 3:10–11).
4. Sacrificial love and commitment (Phil. 2:7–8).

V. Understanding the relationship in marriage in the context of Christ and His Church.

➤ It is unique.
➤ It is exclusive.
➤ It must be subject to the will of God.

The Mystery of Christ and the Church
Ephesians 5:32

I. Context: Jesus told His disciples in John 16:7 "for if I go not away, the Comforter will not come unto you; but if I depart, I will send him unto you." Jesus told His disciples the Comforter would guide them into all truth, but at that time the Holy Spirit, the Spirit of Christ, did not indwell the believers, and their understanding was limited. Truth and understanding for the believer, the Church, the body of Christ came when Jesus ascended back to heaven and the day of Pentecost came. This is the position of the believer during the Church age as stated in Colossians 1:27: "To whom God would make known what is the riches of the glory of this mystery among the Gentiles, which is Christ in you the hope of glory." With the Church being both the body and bride of Christ and Christ indwelling each member of that body, how can that relationship be described? How are the riches of God's glory revealed through this relationship? First, the believer must understand what it means to be a part of the body of Christ. Second, the believer should understand what it means for that body, the Church, to be the bride of Christ. Third, the believer should understand the relationship between Christ and the Church in the context of a Christian marriage. In Ephesians 5:21–32, Paul speaks of Christian marriage as it relates to Christ and the Church. In verse 32, "this is a great mystery, but I speak concerning Christ and the Church."

II. What the Scripture Says About the Body of Christ*:* Church age believers make up the body of Christ, which is a spiritual union that occurs only when a person receives Jesus as Lord and Savior. As Peter speaks of the suffering of Christ for our sins, he says, "For Christ also hath once suffered for sins, the just for the unjust, that he might bring us to God, being put to death in the flesh but made alive by the Spirit" (1 Pet. 3:18). Paul emphasizes that spiritual union in Colossians 2:13: "And you, being dead in your sins and the uncircumcision of your flesh, hath he made alive together with him, having forgiven you all trespasses." Being made alive through Christ, we are made a part of the body of Christ: "For as the body is one and hath many members, and all the members of that one body, being many are one body, so also is Christ. For by one Spirit were we all baptized into one body whether we be Jews or Greeks whether we be bond or free; and have been all made to drink into one Spirit. For the body is not one member, but many" (1 Cor. 12:12–14).

As a believer in Christ Jesus, you give up your carnal rights. You are not your own! "What, Know ye not that your body is the temple of the Holy Spirit who is in you, whom ye have of God, and ye are not your own?" (1 Cor. 6:19). The believer should be dead to the old life by yielding to God through the power of the Holy Spirit. "Likewise, reckon ye also yourselves to be dead indeed unto sin, but alive unto God through Jesus Christ, our Lord. Let not sin therefore, reign in your mortal body, that ye should obey it in lusts" (Rom. 6:11–12).

As a part of the body of Christ, what should the believer understand? (*How does that apply to a Christian marriage relationship?*)

1. Christ is the head of the Church, and the Church is the body of Christ.
2. As a believer in Christ Jesus, you are part of His body.
3. The believer is part of the body of Christ by the power of the Holy Spirit (the Spirit of Christ).
4. The believer's actions are to support the purpose of the whole body, not an isolated member.
5. Sin and self should not rule a believer's life.
6. As a believer you are not your own; you do not make decisions or act in isolation.
7. All that a believer does should edify the whole body of Christ, the Church.

II. What the Scripture Says about the Bride of Christ: The scripture provides no ambiguity as to who the wife, the bride of Christ, is. It is explicit: "Husbands, love your wives, even as Christ also loved the church, and gave himself for it; That he might sanctify and cleanse it with the washing of water by the word. That he might present it to himself a glorious church, not having spot, or wrinkle, or any such thing; but that it should be holy and without blemish" (Eph. 5:25–27). Revelation 21:9 further identifies the Church as the bride of Christ. The Church is the Lamb's wife. In Revelation 19:7–9. details are given of the marriage of Christ and the Church:

> "Let us be glad and rejoice and give honor to him; for the marriage of the Lamb is come, and his wife hath made herself ready. And to her was granted that she should be arrayed in fine linen, clean and white for the fine linen is the righteousness of the saints. And he saith unto me, Write, Blessed are they who are called unto the marriage supper of the Lamb. And he saith unto me, These are the true sayings of God."

The righteousness of saints clearly indicates these are the Church-age saints. The righteousness Jesus gave to the Church is His righteousness. "For he hath made him to be sin for us, who knew no sin; that *we* might be made the righteousness of God in him" (2 Cor. 5:21). The Church is clean, pure, and white because of the righteousness of God through the blood sacrifice of Jesus Christ.

Those called to the Marriage Supper are Old Testament saints. John the Baptist, the last of the Old Testament prophets, was a friend of the bride. "He that hath the bride is the bridegroom; but the friend of the bridegroom which standeth and heareth him, rejoiceth greatly because of the bridegroom's voice: this my joy therefore is fulfilled" (John 3:29). John the Baptist will be a joyous guest of the groom while the apostle John will be a part of the Church, the bride of Christ. John was so overwhelmed by the message, marriage, and praise that he fell at the angel's feet to worship him but was prevented by the angel (Rev. 19:10).

As part of the bride of Christ, what should the believer understand? *(How does that apply to a Christian marriage relationship?)*

1. The believer should understand just how much Christ loves the Church.
2. The believer should understand just how much Christ desires the Church to be pure and clean in all things upon this earth.
3. The believer should understand just how committed Christ is to His bride and the marriage.

IV. The Mystery of Christ and the Church Exemplified by Christian Marriage: In Ephesians 5:21–33, Paul uses the marriage between a Christian man and women to illustrate the relationship between Christ and the Church. As Paul describes the marriage relationship between believers, the biblical standard is clearly Christ and the church: "For this cause shall a man leave his father and mother, and shall be joined unto his wife, and they two shall be one flesh. This is a great mystery, but I speak concerning Christ and the church" (Eph. 5:31). Just as God's model for the church is grounded in *unity, order, commitment, and love*, so is marriage between a Christian man and woman. Unity and order are demonstrated by the seven principles the believer should understand as being a part of the body of Christ. Commitment and love are demonstrated by the three principles a believer should understand as part of what Christ did for His bride, the Church.

First, *unity and order* are illustrated in a Christian marriage by the actions of the wife. Ephesians 5:22 states: "Wives, submit yourselves unto your own husbands, as unto the Lord." So, what is the Greek word for submit, and what does it mean? According to *Strong's Exhaustive Concordance of the Bible* by James Strong and the *Expository Dictionary of New Testament Words* by W.E. Vine, the Greek word is *hupeiko* (νπείκω), and the word means to put under, to subordinate, to be subject to, submit self to. The believer is to recognize that Christ is the head of the Church, and the Church is the body of Christ made up of many believers. Therefore, in Christian marriage, the husband and wife are one body, one flesh. Just as the believer is one of many members in the body of Christ, in a Christian marriage, there are two, yet one flesh, one spiritual body that should act in unity. Submission "as unto the Lord" is a very lofty position that can only be attained by the power of the Holy Spirit for both the husband and wife.

Just as unity in the Church comes about by the power of the Holy Spirit, it will come in the same way in Christian marriage. In Ephesians 4:3–6, Paul encourages the unity of the Church: "Endeavoring to keep the unity of the Spirit in the bond of peace. There is one body, and one Spirit even as ye are called in one hope of your calling; One Lord, one faith, one baptism, One God and Father of all, who is above all and through all, and in you all." Just as each believer is to support the purpose of the whole Church body, the husband and wife should support the marriage in unity, not serving self, not making decisions in isolation without the spouse. As each believer is equipped with spiritual gifts to edify the Church, so is the husband and wife equipped to edify the marriage in different ways. The order of the godhead is Father, Son, and Holy Spirit. The order of the marriage relationship is husband, wife, and children. God intended unity and order in the Christian marriage, but it will not be attained if God is left out of the marriage relationship.

Second, *love and commitment* are illustrated in Christian marriage by the husband. In Ephesians 5:25: "Husbands, love your wives, even as Christ also loved the church, and gave himself for it." So, what kind of love is Paul talking about? The Greek word used for love is *agapao* (ἀγαπάω).[11] It describes the attitude of God toward His Son. It is used to convey God's will to His children concerning their attitude toward

---

[11]   W.E. Vine, *An Expository Dictionary of New Testament Words*.

one another and toward all men, and it is used to express the essential nature of God. Christian love, hence the love of the husband, has God for its primary object, and expresses itself first of all in implicit obedience to His commandments. Self-will is the negation of love to God.[12] Christian love is the fruit of the Holy Spirit in the Christian (Gal. 5:2). Therefore, for a husband to love his wife with this kind of love, he must be a believer. The reference to submission and love Paul speaks of only applies to believers, *not* the world, for the lost world cannot understand the love of God.

Christ's love for the Church came first and is unbounded. He gave himself to redeem the Church. He is now sanctifying the Church (Eph. 5:26). Christ's love for the Church is also future in that He will present His bride to Himself without spot or blemish (v. 27). With His blood, Jesus purchased the Pearl of Great Price (Matt. 13:46). Just how much did Christ love the Church? He died for every believer who makes up His body. That kind of love cannot be attained and demonstrated by the husband except by the power of the Holy Spirit. Christ's love for His bride is precious and so should the love of a husband for his wife.

The love and commitment of Christ for His Church is demonstrated by His *willingness* to go to the cross. Jesus said "not my will but thine be done" (Luke 22:42). Jesus knew the pain and suffering He was about to go through. Yet, He was totally committed before the foundations of the world (1 Pet. 1:19–20). "But God commandeth his love toward us in that, while we were yet sinners, Christ died for us" (Rom. 5:8). "We love him, because he first loved us" (John 4:19). The love by the husband for the wife should be willful and not subject to the whims of feelings. Hurt feelings causes disunity and can destroy a marriage.

---

[12]   Ibid.

Christ's love and commitment were *purposed*. God's will may not be done because He desires all to come to a saving knowledge of Christ Jesus (Matt. 18:11–14), but they will not and Christ will tell many to "depart from me ye cursed, into everlasting fire, prepared for the devil and his angels." (Matt. 25:41). However, His purpose is eternal and will be done (Eph. 3:10–11). The husband should purpose to treat his wife as if the treatment came from God.

Christ's love and commitment were *sacrificial*. Jesus was obedient to death, even the death of the cross (Phil. 2:7–8). Sometimes there are rifts within the marriage. The rifts may occur because of the unwillingness of one to sacrifice for the other. When Christian husbands and wives think of the triviality of most issues compared to the sacrifice of Jesus, we should be ashamed.

V. Understanding the Relationship: Christ commitment to His bride, the church, is *unique* in every way. He loved His bride before she knew Him or had any desire for Him. He alone has paid the price for her purity. He has equipped His bride with spiritual gifts for continued sanctification that she might be transformed into a pure, clean body, fit for the King of kings. The commitment is *exclusive* in that Christ is not through with the church but is constantly guiding and watching over her by His Word. There is nothing else in creation like it. The commitment by the husband should be exclusive and unique to that couple under the umbrella of God's Word. The wife submits as the Church submits to the lordship of Christ. The husband loves the wife as if it is Christ who is behind every action of the husband toward the wife. Then, *submission and love* create a marriage that reflects the mystery of Christ and the Church.

Chapter 5

The Mystery of the Resurrection

1 Corinthians 15:1–51

I. Context:

- ➢ The heresy of no resurrection of the dead.
- ➢ An overview of the context of the resurrection.

II. The Gospel declared to the Church at Corinth (1 Cor. 15:1–11)

- ➢ The Gospel of God's grace preached by Paul.
- ➢ What Paul received he delivered.

    1. Christ died for our sins according to the scriptures.
    2. Christ was buried and rose again the third day according to the scriptures.

- ➢ Christ was seen by many after His resurrection.
- ➢ By the grace of God, Paul preached the gospel of grace.

III. How some say there is no resurrection? (1 Cor. 15:12–19)

- ➢ Without the resurrection, Christianity is vain (useless, empty, void of result).

➢ Mankind is still in sin.

➢ All men are most miserable.

IV. *The order of the resurrection:*

➢ Resurrected to physically die again.

1. Old Testament people were raised from the dead (2 Kings 4:32–35; 13:21).
2. Jesus raised Lazarus from the dead (John 11:43–44; Luke 7:12–15).
3. Peter raised Tabitha (Dorcas) from the dead (Acts 9:36–42).

➢ The first resurrection unto life; those with a glorified body (John 5:25–29)

1. Believed by Job (Job 19:25–27).
2. Prophesied by Isaiah and Daniel (Isa. 26:19, Dan. 12:2).
3. Jesus Christ, the first fruits of them that slept. (1 Cor. 15:22–23).
4. Old Testament saints after the crucifixion, death, and resurrection of Christ. (Matt. 27:52–53).
5. Old Testament and Church age saints. (1 Thess. 4:14–17; Rev. 20:4–6).
6. At the end of the tribulation (Rev. 20:4–6).

➢ The second resurrection of damnation (John 5:29; Rev. 20:11:12).

V. *The resurrected spiritual body will not die again (1 Cor. 15:35–50)*

➢ Different bodies that God gives (v. 38)?

1. Example of a seed. The plant dies then the seed is planted and is raised.
2. There are different glories of the bodies:

   a. All flesh is not the same: Man, beasts, fish, birds.
   b. Celestial and terrestrial bodies: Sun, Moon, Stars.

➤ So, what body of the dead will be resurrected?

1. Sown in corruption, raised in incorruption.
2. Sown in dishonor, raised in glory.
3. Sown a natural body, raised a spiritual body.
4. Adam a living soul, Christ a life-giving spirit.
5. Natural man always precedes spiritual man.
6. Flesh and blood, natural man, cannot inherit the kingdom of God.

VI. What about those who do not die? (1 Cor. 15:51–53)

➤ Not all sleep (die) but are changed (v. 51).
➤ Changed quickly, in the twinkling of an eye (v. 52).
➤ At the last trump. (v. 52). The Greek word for trump is *salpinx* (σάλπιγε). "The act of the Lord in raising from the dead the saints who have fallen asleep and changing the bodies of those who are living, at the rapture of all to meet Him in the air where "the last trump" is a military allusion, familiar to Greek readers, and has no connection to the trumpet judgments of Revelation 8:6–11:15.[13]"
➤ Corruptible will put on incorruption and mortal will put on immortality.

---

[13] Ibid.

VII. What about those who are in the grave? (1 Thess. 4:15–17).

➢ Paul is explaining to the believers at Thessalonica what will happen to their Christian loved ones who have died.

1. The Lord Jesus will descend from heaven with a shout, with the voice of the archangel, and with the trump of God. (The same trump as in 1 Corinthians 15:52).
2. The dead in Christ will be resurrected with a glorified body before those who are alive will be caught up (v. 15).
3. Believers who are alive at that time will be caught up together with them in the clouds to meet the Lord in the air; and will ever be with the Lord.

➢ Thessalonian believers are to comfort each other with this spiritual truth (v. 18).

VIII. The Church will not be on earth during the Tribulation.

➢ God has not appointed the Church to wrath (1 Thess. 5:9).
➢ God will keep the Church from the hour of temptation (Rev. 3:10).
➢ The three songs of validation.

IX. The Second Resurrection: No one will be singing.

X. Summary: Raised and Changed.

The Mystery of the Resurrection
1 Corinthians 15:51

I. Context: Sound fundamental Bible doctrine emphasizes the resurrection of the dead. Paul delt emphatically with this doctrine in his letter to the Corinthians. Heresy had surfaced among some as revealed by Paul's letter to the Corinthian church in 1 Corinthians 15:12; "Now if Christ be preached that he rose from the dead, how say some among you that there is no resurrection of the dead?" In dealing with the heresy, Paul decisively lays out the argument and introduces another mystery that has been discussed and debated for centuries among believers. The mystery goes beyond just a bodily resurrection. It challenges the believer to research and understand the resurrection in the context of position, timing, and type. Position meaning where one stands before Christ Jesus as either a believer or unbeliever. Timing means the order of the resurrections, and type means with a body like that of Christ Jesus, a glorified body, or a body like unto Lazarus who Jesus raised, yet would die again. Paul points to the mystery of the resurrection in 1 Corinthians 15:51 when he says, *"Behold, I show you a mystery: We shall not all sleep but we shall all be changed, in a moment, in the twinkling of an eye, at the last trump for the trumpet shall sound, and the dead shall be raised incorruptible and we shall be changed."*

There are events, songs, gospels, promises, identities, and Church periods that Jesus and the apostles, by the power of the Holy Spirit, revealed to believers who seek to understand the mystery of the resurrection. A topical list is now provided that will help put the pieces of the resurrection mystery puzzle together, and will be discussed in detail as the other mysteries are revealed:

1. **ONE RAPTURE of the Church**: 1 Thessalonians 4:16–17. The dead first and then those who are alive.

2. **TWO RESURRECTIONS:** John 5: 25–29. Resurrection of life and resurrection of damnation.

3. **THREE SONGS:** Song of the Old Testament saints and the raptured Church (Rev. 5:9–10), Song of the 144,000 Jews who preached during the tribulation (Rev. 14:3), and Song of the Jews and Gentiles saved during the tribulation (Rev. 7:14; 15:3).

4. **FOUR GOSPELS:** *Of the kingdom* (Matt. 24:14), *of grace* (Acts 20:24), *of Paul* (Rom. 2:16), *everlasting gospel* (Rev. 14:5). Reference the *mystery of the gospel.*

5. **FIVE PROMISES:** The Church *will not* be in the tribulation (1 Thess. 5:9; Rev. 3:10), new body (1 Cor. 15:53), no sorrow for the deceased (1 Thess. 4:13), swift transition (1 Cor. 15:52), seeing Jesus, fellowship (1 Thess. 4:17)

6. **SIXS OF SATAN:** Satan's counterfeit of the Trinity (666, the Dragon, the Beast, the False Prophet) all incomplete and imperfect (Rev. 13:1–18)

7. **SEVEN CHURCH PERIODS:** Reference the *Mystery of the Seven Stars* and the *Seven Golden Lampstands.*

II. The Gospel Declared to the Church at Corinth (1 Cor. 15:1–22): Paul begins to deal with the heresy by reminding the Corinthians what they had already experienced. Paul had preached the *Gospel of grace* to the Corinthians. They had believed and were saved as they were now standing in God's grace and on His promises. Paul tells them that the death, burial, and resurrection of Jesus was all according to the scripture. Paul emphasizes the witnesses to the resurrected Lord and Savior. There was Peter, the twelve, over five-hundred at one time, James and all the apostles, and finally Paul himself who met the resurrected Lord Jesus on the road to Damascus. Paul would vividly remember the encounter as he too was saved and set apart as an apostle to the Gentiles. Paul tells the Corinthians, "But by the grace of God I am what I am; and his grace, which was bestowed upon me, was not in vain, but I labored more abundantly than they all; yet not I, but the grace of God which was with me." Paul labored then and would labor the rest of his life on earth sharing the *Gospel of grace* to a lost world.

III. How Some Say There is no Resurrection? (1 Cor. 15:12–19): Paul points out to the Corinthian believers just how serious and destructive the concept of no bodily resurrection would be to the gospel. The gospel of Jesus Christ would not be good news but a miserable state for the believer. Paul presents a series of questions that would logically show the Corinthian Christians just how flawed the thought of no resurrection would be and the end result of such a doctrinal belief. He presents these in a series of if/then statements:

1. *If* no resurrection from the dead, *then* is Christ not risen.
2. *If* Christ is not risen, *then* our preaching is in vain.
3. *If* our preaching is in vain, *then* your faith is also in vain.
4. *If* the preaching of the resurrection is in vain, *then* we are found false witnesses of God.
5. *If* we are false witnesses of God, *then* the dead rise not.
6. *If* the dead rise not, *then* Christ is not risen.
7. *If* Christ is not raised, *then* your faith is in vain.
8. *If* your faith is in vain, *then* you are yet in your sins.
9. *If* we are yet in our sin and there is no resurrection, *then* those dead (fallen asleep) in Christ are perished.
10. *If* in this life only we have hope in Christ, *then* we are of all men most miserable (v. 19).

IV. First, the Order of the Resurrection cannot be understood without an understanding of the type of body the believer will receive. This is demonstrated in Old Testament scripture by Elisha raising the Shunammite's son from the dead (2 Kings 4:32–35). The boy was raised to live again in a natural body but would die again. It was demonstrated by the raising of Dorcas from the dead by Peter (Acts 9:36–42). Dorcus would die again. Finally, Jesus raised Lazarus from the dead, not with a glorified body, but a natural body that would die again (John 11:43–44). When Jesus told Martha "Thy brother shall rise again. Martha saith unto him, I know that he shall rise again in the resurrection at the last day" (John 11:23–26). Martha was speaking of the resurrection of the believer in the last day: "Blessed and holy is he that hath part in the first resurrection; on such the second death hath no power, but they shall be priests of God and of Christ, and shall reign with him a thousand years (Rev. 20:6). However, Jesus was speaking of both the immediate resurrection of Lazarus back to his natural body and the resurrection at the last day. Jesus raised Lazarus's natural body so that Martha would see the glory of God and people would believe Jesus was sent by the Father (John 11:40, 42). Lazarus would physically die again but the resurrection of his new body would be eternal (John 11:26). This is the last resurrection that Jesus spoke of and that Martha understood. Jesus said: "And whosoever liveth and believeth in me shall never die. Believest thou this?" The last resurrection that Dorcus and Lazarus would experience would be the resurrection of a spiritual body (1 Cor. 15:44).

Second, the order of the resurrection depends upon what Jesus told us concerning *two resurrections.* In John 5:28–29, Jesus said: "Marvel not at this; for the hour is coming, in which all that are in the graves shall hear his voice, And shall come forth: they that have done good, unto the *resurrection of life;* and they that have done evil, unto the *resurrection of damnation.*

The Old Testament saints believed in the resurrection. Job believed and said in Job 19:25–27: "For I know that my redeemer liveth, and that he shall stand at the latter day upon the earth; And though after my skin worms destroy this body, yet in my flesh shall I see God, Whom I shall see for myself, and mine eyes shall behold, and not another; though my heart be consumed within me." Isaiah prophesied of the bodily resurrection: "Thy dead men shall live together with my dead body shall they arise. Awake and sing, ye that dwell in dust; for thy dew is like the dew of herbs, and the earth shall cast out the dead" (Isa. 26:19). Daniel speaks of the two resurrections in Daniel 12:2: "And many of those who sleep in the dust of the earth shall awake, some to everlasting life, and some to shame and everlasting contempt."

The first resurrection, the resurrection of life, occurred and will continue to occur in the following order.

1. *Jesus Christ, the first fruits of them that slept* (1 Cor. 15:20–23), "But now is Christ risen from the dead and become the first fruits of them that slept … But every man is his own order; Christ the first fruits; afterward they that are Christ's at his coming."

2. *Old Testament saints after the resurrection of Christ* (Matt. 27:52–53) "And the graves were opened; and many bodies of the saints that slept were raised, And came out of the graves after his resurrection, and went into the holy city, and appeared unto many."

3. *Old Testament and Church age saints at the coming of Christ in the air* (1 Thess. 4:16–18; Rev. 5:9). "For the Lord himself shall descend from heaven with a shout, with the voice of the archangel, and with the trump of God; and the dead in Christ shall rise first; Then we who are alive and remain shall be caught up together with them in the clouds to meet the Lord in the air; and so shall we ever be with the Lord. Wherefore,

comfort one another with these words." (1 Thess. 4:16–18). These are seen by John singing a new song in heaven (Rev. 5:9).

4. *Believers who were beheaded for refusing to worship the Beast at the end of the tribulation:* (Rev. 20:4–6), "And I saw thrones, and they sat upon them, and judgement was given unto them; and I saw the souls of them that were beheaded for the witness of Jesus, and for the word of God, and who had not worshiped the beast, neither his image, neither had received his mark upon their foreheads, or in their hands; and they lived and reigned with Christ a thousand years. But the rest of the dead lived not again until the thousand years were finished. This is the first resurrection. Blessed and holy is he that hath part in the first resurrection; on such the second death hath no power, but they shall be priests of God and of Christ, and shall reign with him a thousand years."

Each of these events constitute the first resurrection to life. It begins with the resurrection of Jesus Christ and will end with those believers who were martyred at the end of the tribulation period.

After the thousand-year reign of Christ, *the second resurrection of damnation will occur.*

"At that time, the dead, small and great, will stand before the great white throne to be judged by Jesus Christ. The sea, death, and hades will deliver up the dead for their judgment. They will be judged according to their works. And death and hades were cast into the lake of fire." This is the second death. And whosoever was not found written in the book of life was cast into the lake of fire. (Rev. 20:11–15)

V. The Resurrected Spiritual Body Will Not Die Again: So, what is the mystery? Is it the spiritual body that the believer receives? Paul addresses the question of how the dead are raised and the type of body received by them in 1 Corinthians 15:35–50. "But some man will say, How are the dead raised up? And with what body do they come? Thou fool, that which thou sowest is not made alive, except it die." The example of a seed (maybe a wheat seed) is used. Wheat is a green plant in late winter and early spring. The plant grows and changes from a green short plant to a long-stem stalk. The stalk puts on seed and turns brown in the fall as the seed ripens. The stalk dies, leaving the grain to be harvested. Some of the lifeless seed will be planted to bring forth again a vibrant green plant. Paul illustrates, as the seed cycle is described to have different bodies, God also gives other parts of His creation different bodies. The flesh of man, beast, fish, and birds, which are alive are different. The glory of the sun, moon, and stars are different.

The examples by Paul are given to illustrate a comparison to the resurrection of the believer. "So also is the resurrection of the dead. It is sown in corruption; it is raised in incorruption. It is sown in dishonor; it is raised in glory. It is sown in weakness; it is raised in power. It is sown a natural body; it is raised a spiritual body; There is a natural body, and there is a spiritual body" (1 Cor. 15:42–44). Using the life of Adam and the eternal Christ, Paul shows natural man will come before spiritual man, and Adam was of the earth where the Lord is from heaven. All of mankind has born the image of Adam (sinful, terminal, earthly), but believers will be resurrected to bear the image of the heavenly, *a spiritual, glorified body.*

VI. What About Those Who Do Not Die? What Is the Mystery? Is it the glorified body of the believer *or* is it that some believers will not die and will receive a spiritual, glorified body? This question leads to one of the most studied and debated topics of the New

Testament. What did the Holy Spirit reveal to Paul when he wrote: "Behold, I show you a mystery: We shall not all sleep, but we shall all be changed, In a moment, in the twinkling of an eye, at the last trump. For the trumpet shall sound, and the dead shall be raised incorruptible, and we shall be changed. For this corruptible must put on incorruption, and this mortal must put on immortality" (1 Cor. 15:51–53)? Paul gave sufficient context as to the resurrection and the type of body the believer will receive. However, when Paul says we shall not all sleep (Greek idiom for die) and shall be changed, much more context is needed. Peter warned the believer not to study God's Word in isolation but to look at the entire biblical context: "Knowing this first, that no prophecy of the scripture is of any private interpretation" (2 Pet. 1:20). Much more context is needed and provided by Paul in his letters to the church at Thessalonica and John's prophecy of the Revelation of Jesus Christ.

VI. What About Those Who Are in the Grave? Believers in the church of Thessalonica were concerned for their Christian loved ones who had died. Their desire was to know what was to become of them as it related to the resurrection. In 1 Thessalonians 4:15–17, Paul comforts them with these words:

> "But I would not have you ignorant, brethren, concerning them who are asleep, that ye sorrow not, even as others who have no hope. For if we believe that Jesus died and rose again, even so them also who sleep in Jesus will God bring with him. For this we say unto you by the word of the Lord, that we who are alive and remain unto the coming of the Lord shall not precede them who are asleep. For the Lord himself shall descend from heaven with a shout, with the voice of the archangel, and with the trump of God; and the dead in Christ shall rise first; Then we who

are alive and remain shall be caught up together with them in the clouds, to meet the Lord in the air; and so shall we ever be with the Lord. Wherefore, comfort one another with these words."

From these verses, Paul presents four very important doctrinal points:

1. The apostles, including Paul, were providing the doctrine not as conjecture but by the word of the Lord. It was what God had shown them!

2. In the resurrection, those who would be alive when the event happened would not go before those believers who were in the grave.

3. The Lord will descend from heaven, but not to the earth.

4. The believers who are alive will be caught up in the clouds to meet Jesus in the air. The short word for the Church to be "caught up" is rapture. There is *one rapture* of the *Church* as John's prophecy reveals.

VIII. The Church Will Not Be On Earth During the Tribulation! It Will Be Raptured! The Trump of God will sound as Paul states in letters to both the churches and other believers. It will happen immediately. Those who are caught up will receive a spiritual, glorified body. So, who is caught up? We find the answer revealed by John's prophecy in the Revelation of Jesus Christ. In Revelation, there are *three songs* and three events that provide the key to the mystery of the resurrection. These keys firmly point to the fact that Christ *will not* put his bride, the Church, through the tribulation period. The biblical background now follows:

In Revelation 4:4, a vision of the throne of God and those that surround it are given; "And round about the throne were four and twenty thrones, and upon the thrones I saw four and twenty elders sitting, clothed in white raiment; and they had on their heads crowns of gold. Who are the elders? Why are they wearing white, and why are they sitting on thrones and wearing crowns of gold? *The elders represent the church* (1 Tim; 5:17; Titus 1:5). The white raiment represents purity because they have been raised from the dead, incorruptible, and have walked with Jesus (Rev. 3:4). The thrones are associated with judgment because believers will judge the world and angels: "Do ye not know that the saints shall judge the world: And if the world shall be judged by you, are ye unworthy to judge the smallest matters? Know ye not that we shall judge angels: How much more things that pertain to this life?" (1 Cor. 6:2,3) (This will be prevalent during the thousand-year reign of Christ). The crowns represent the rewards for the faithful in the church: A crown of rejoicing (1 Thess, 2:19), a crown of righteousness (2 Tim, 4:8), a crown of life (James 1:12), a crown of glory (1 Pet, 5:4). What John saw in heaven at this time was the resurrected (raptured) Church.

Later, in Revelation 5:8–10, the elders are present as well as a host of saints out of every kindred, tongue, people and nation *singing a new song.* They are singing a new song, saying Christ is worthy to take the seven-sealed scroll and open it. They are praising him as our Redeemer and Savior. The messages to the churches have been completed; no seal at this time had been opened, and no judgment had yet been unleased. The timing indicates the Church is in heaven (one rapture) before Christ opens any of the seals, triggering the beginning of the tribulation period.

Further biblical evidence that the Church will not be subject to the tribulation period is found in in 1 Thessalonians 5:9. Paul was speaking of the Church being caught up in chapter 4 and after a series of conjunctions states, "For God hath not appointed us to wrath but to obtain salvation by our Lord Jesus Christ." In Revelation, the Lord Jesus instructed the angel to tell John concerning the message to Philadelphia: "Because thou hast kept the word of my patience, I also will keep thee from the hour of temptation, which shall come upon all the world, to try them that dwell upon the earth" (Rev. 3:9). The messages to the churches (Rev. 2 and 3) represent *seven Church periods* with Philadelphia preceding Laodicea, the church in its final state of apostasy. Finally, when studying the mystery of Christ and the Church, the bride of Christ, it is inconceivable that Christ would put His bride through hell on earth (Rev. 19:7–9). *This is the rapture,* the resurrection of the Church and the Old Testament saints that Paul was speaking of in 1 Corinthians 15:51–53 and 1 Thessalonians 4:13–18. *The first song* and its associated resurrection is complete.

The *second song* will be sung by the 144,000 Jews who will preach to every nation, kindred, people, and tongue (Rev. 7:1–15). They will not be preaching the Gospel of grace, but will be preaching the Gospel of the kingdom, fulfilling the prophecy of Jesus when He said. "And this gospel of the kingdom shall be preached in all the world for a witness unto the nations; and then shall the end come" (Matt. 24:14). No one but the 144,000 Jews could learn this new song (Rev. 14:3). They had been martyred by the counterfeit trinity, *the sixes of Satan* (The Dragon a 6, Satan; The Beast a 6, the man of sin, the son of perdition, the Antichrist; and The False Prophet a 6). The 144,000 have been resurrected to be with and follow the Lamb (Jesus) in heaven (Rev. 14:4). These are part of the group that will be resurrected at the end of the tribulation.

The *Third Song* is sung by those who received the Gospel of the kingdom preached by the 144,000 Jews and were martyred by the sixes of Satan. They were seen by John and identified by the elder to John in Revelation 7:14 as those who came out of the great tribulation. The song they sing is not new: "And they sing the song of Moses, the servant of God, and the song of the Lamb saying Great and marvelous are thy works, Lord God Almighty; just and true are thy ways, thou King of saints" (Rev. 15:3). It is the song of Moses, representing the Jews saved during the tribulation and the song of the Lamb representing the Gentiles saved during the tribulation. The third song represents the last group to be included in the first resurrection: the resurrection of life.

The three songs are important because they represent different people, time periods, and events. If the resurrection of the Church and the martyrs of the tribulation are at the same time, there would be no need for a third song. If the Church were part of the tribulation period, preaching the Gospel of the Kingdom, they too could sing the song of the 144,000 Jews.

IX. Then Comes the Second Resurrection, the Resurrection of Damnation, and No One Will Be Singing. "And the sea gave up the dead that were in it, and death and hades delivered up the dead that were in them; and they were judged every man according to their works. And death and hades were cast into the lake of fire. This is the second death. And whosoever was not found written in the book of life was cast into the lake of fire" (Rev. 20:14–15).

X. Summary: There are five events in the two resurrections. There are four in the resurrection of life and one in the resurrection of damnation. There is no mystery implied with the resurrection of Jesus, the first fruits. There is no mystery implied with the Old Testament believers raised after Jesus arose, who went into Jerusalem and appeared to many. There is no mystery implied with the resurrection of the 144,000 Jews who preached the Gospel of the kingdom and the Jews and Gentiles resurrected at the end of the tribulation. The resurrection of those damned to the lake of fire for rejecting

Jesus is surely not a mystery. The Bible is very clear when it comes to the consequences of rejecting Jesus as Lord and Savior. That leaves either the rapture of the Church as the mystery, or the glorified body as the mystery, or both. I believe it is both: The Church made up of both deceased and living saintsraised and changed!

Chapter 6

The Mystery of the Gospel

Ephesians 6:19

I. **Context:**

- ➤ Matthew, Mark. Luke and John written for specific audiences.
- ➤ The four gospels are not the mystery.

II. **Paul preached boldly the Mystery of the Gospel. (Eph. 6:19)**

- ➤ God's promise of Good News; all families of the earth blessed (Gen. 12:1–3).
- ➤ God's promise (covenant with King David; 2 Sam. 7:16).
- ➤ It is the Gospel of Christ (John 1:12–13).

III. **The order of the Mystery of the Gospel:**

- ➤ Gospel of the kingdom (Matt. 24:14).
- ➤ Gospel of the grace of God (Acts 20:24).
- ➤ The everlasting gospel (Rev. 14:6).
- ➤ Paul's (my gospel) Gospel of grace (Rom. 2:16).
- ➤ Another gospel, a perversion of the Gospel of grace (Gal. 1:6–7).

IV. Gospel of the Kingdom: (Matt. 24:14)

1. Starts with John the Baptist, continued by Jesus and his disciples (Mark 1:1–4, 14–15; Matt. 4:23). The seventy sent forth (Luke 10:1–12).
2. Ends with the rejection of Jesus by the Jews (Isa. 53:3; Matt. 23:37–39).
3. Starts again during the tribulation (Rev. 7:4–17).
4. Ends at the second coming of Jesus Christ (Matt. 24:14; Luke 21:24). Time of the Gentiles to be fulfilled.

V. Gospel of the Grace of God (Gospel of God, Rom. 1:1; Gospel of Christ, 2 Cor. 10:14).

➤ God's love (John 3:16).
➤ God's sacrifice of His only Son (Isa. 53).
➤ Gospel of the grace of God (Acts: 20:24); God's unmerited mercy (Rom. 9:14–16).
➤ Gospel of our salvation to those that believe (Rom. 1:16).

VI. The Everlasting Gospel (Rev. 14:6–7)

➤ Not the Gospel of the kingdom and not the Gospel of the grace of God!
➤ Preached during the tribulation to all that dwell on the earth (v. 6).
➤ Preached by an angel (v. 6.)
➤ A gospel of judgment. Good for those who trust Jesus (Rev. 7:9); bad for those who worship the Beast (Rev. 14:9–12).

VII. Paul (My Gospel) Gospel of Grace, Personified (Rom. 2:16).

➤ This is the full development of the Gospel of grace represented by all that was proclaimed to the churches Paul established on his missionary journey and sent letters.

➤ The results of Christ establishing His Church showing the Church's position (body of Christ), relationships (bride of Christ), privileges (coming directly to the High Priest, Jesus Christ), and responsibility (study, share, defend the Gospel).

VIII. Another gospel: Not another but perversion of the Gospel of Grace. (2 Cor. 11:4, 13; Gal. 1:6–9)

➤ Warnings by Jesus (Matt. 7:15–16).

➤ Warnings by Paul (Gal. 1:6–9; 1 Tim. 6:20).

➤ Warnings by Peter (2 Pet. 2:2).

The Mystery of the Gospel
Ephesians 6:19

I. Context: When describing the gospel, Matthew, Mark, Luke, and John usually come to mind. The Gospel according to Matthew was originally written for the Jews. The Gospel of Mark was written principally for the Roman world where the Gospel of Luke was written for the Greeks. The purpose of John's gospel was "that ye might believe that Jesus is the Christ, the Son of God; and believing ye might have life through his name" (John 20:31). The four gospels are not the mystery that Paul speaks of in Ephesians 6:19.

II. Paul Desired to Preach Boldly the Mystery of the Gospel "And for me, that utterance may be given unto me, that I may open my mouth boldly to make known the mystery of the gospel" (Eph. 6:19).

The Greek word for Gospel is *euangelion* (εναγγέλτον), meaning good news. The good news was first delivered by God to Abram.

> "Now the LORD had said unto Abram, Get thee out of thy country, and from thy Kindred, and from thy father's house, unto a land that I will show thee; And I will make of thee a great nation, and I will bless thee and make thy name great; and thou shalt be a blessing. And I will bless them that bless thee, and curse him that curseth thee: and in thee shall all families of the earth be blessed." (Gen. 12:1–3)

The good news went far beyond Abram and his immediate family. The good news extended to the creation of a nation fathered by Abram, a house and kingdom that would be established forever through his descendent, King David, and by Jesus Christ ("And thine house and thy kingdom shall be established forever before thee; thy throne shall be established forever" (2 Sam. 7:16) and all the families of the earth would be blessed. The families of the earth would be blessed with the coming of the Savior, Christ the Lord. "But as many as received him, to them gave he power to become the children of God, even to them that believe on his name; Who were born, not of blood, nor of the will of the flesh, nor of the will of man, but of God" (John1:12–13).

III. The Order of the Gospel: Just as good news had come to Abraham, King David, and the prophets, the remaining gospels would come dispensationally:

1. Jesus spoke of the *Gospel of the kingdom*. "And this gospel of the kingdom shall be preached in all the world for a witness unto the nations; and then shall the end come" (Matt. 24:14)

2. Paul spoke of the *Gospel of the grace* of God. "But none of these things move me, neither count I my life dear unto myself, so that I might finish my course with joy, and ministry, which I have received of the Lord Jesus to testify the gospel of the grace of God" (Acts 20:24).

3. John spoke of the *everlasting Gospel*. "And I saw another angel fly in the midst of heaven, having the everlasting gospel to preach unto them that dwell on the earth, and to every nation, and kindred and tongue, and people" (Rev. 14:6).

4. Paul also spoke of *"my gospel."* "In the day when God shall judge the secrets of men by Jesus Christ according to my gospel" (Rom. 2:16).

5. Paul also speaks of *another gospel*. "I marvel that ye are so removed from him that called you into the grace of Christ unto another gospel: Which is not another; but there be some that trouble you, and would pervert the gospel of Christ" (Gal. 1:6–7).

The chart below gives a depiction of the time line of these gospels:

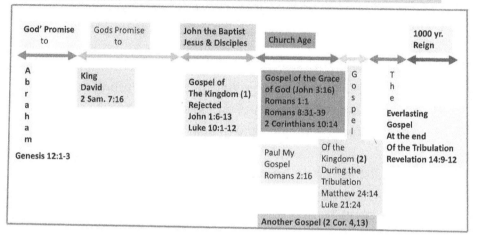

The Mystery of the Gospel Ephesians 6:19

God' Promise to	Gods Promise to	John the Baptist Jesus & Disciples	Church Age	1000 yr. Reign

A b r a h a m	King David 2 Sam. 7:16	Gospel of The Kingdom (1) Rejected John 1:6-13 Luke 10:1-12	Gospel of the Grace of God (John 3:16) Romans 1:1 Romans 8:31-39 2 Corinthians 10:14	G o s p e l	T h e Everlasting Gospel At the end Of the Tribulation Revelation 14:9-12
Genesis 12:1-3			Paul My Gospel Romans 2:16	Of the Kingdom (2) During the Tribulation Matthew 24:14 Luke 21:24	

Another Gospel (2 Cor. 4,13)

IV. The Gospel of the Kingdom: will be preached in two different time periods. The first period began with John the Baptist and end with the rejection and crucifixion of Jesus. The second period will begin with the rapture of the Church and end with the return of Jesus at the end of the great tribulation.

The time of the beginning of the Gospel of the kingdom is found in Mark 1:1–4: "The beginning of the gospel of Jesus Christ, the Son of God: As it is written in the prophets, "Behold, I send my messenger before thy face, who shall prepare thy way before thee. The voice of one crying in the wilderness, Prepare ye the way of the Lord, make his paths straight. John did baptize in the wilderness, and preach the baptism of repentance for the remission of sins." John the Baptist's proclamation was followed by the preaching of Jesus. "Now after John was put in prison, Jesus came into Galilee, preaching the gospel of the kingdom of God, And saying, the time is fulfilled, and the kingdom of God is at hand; repent, and believe the gospel" (Mark 1:14–15). "And Jesus went about all Galilee, teaching in their synagogues, and preaching the gospel of the kingdom, and healing all manner of sickness and all manner of disease among the people" (Matt. 4:23). Jesus continued to preach the gospel of the kingdom where ever He went. "And Jesus went about all the cities and villages, teaching in their synagogues, and preaching the gospel of the kingdom, and healing every sickness and every disease among the people" (Matt. 9:35). Jesus also sent forth seventy of his disciples to preach the gospel of the kingdom (Luke 10:1–12).

The gospel of the kingdom ceased being preached when Jesus was rejected and the time of the crucifixion was inevitable (Isa. 53:3). This is marked by the lamentation of Jesus over Jerusalem in Matthew 23:37–39. At this time the gospel of the kingdom had *not* been preached in all the world and to all the nations. The King would be crucified and the kingdom would not be set up. *So, when would there be a second time period for preaching the Gospel of the kingdom and the fulfillment of the prophecy of Jesus (Matt. 24:14)?*

Jesus answers the question as to the fulfillment of the prophecy that He spoke of in Matthew 24. After Jesus lamented over Jerusalem and departed from the temple, His disciples came to Him, speaking of the impressiveness of the temple, and Jesus told them not one stone would be left upon another. It would be totally destroyed. The disciples asked Jesus three questions: When shall these things be? What shall be the sign of thy coming and of the end of the age (Matt. 24:1–3)? Jesus tells His disciples of the beginning of sorrows, persecution, and how iniquity shall abound. Then Jesus said, "And this gospel of the kingdom shall be preached in all the world for a witness unto all nations; and then shall the end come" (Matt. 24:14). The preaching of the gospel of the kingdom was about to be put on hold because the King and the kingdom would not be established at this time. However,

His kingdom will be established when Jesus returns as Lord of lords and King of kings (Rev. 19:11–16). As John the Baptist first preached the Gospel of the kingdom, the 144,000 Jews during the tribulation will preach the Gospel of the kingdom the second time (Rev. 7). The gospel of the kingdom will be loud and clear. It will require a life-and-death commitment. Giving one's life to Jesus may result in a physical death, but their resurrection will be to eternal life. It will not be a cheap gospel. The time between the first proclamation and the second proclamation of the gospel of the kingdom is the full Church age and will end when the times of the Gentiles is fulfilled (Luke 21:24).

V. Gospel of Grace: Paul speaks of the Gospel of God and of Christ when writing to the churches at Rome, Corinth, and Galatia as he presents the Gospel of God, defends his apostolic authority, and warns of the perversion of the gospel of Christ (Rom. 1:1; 2 Cor. 10:14; Gal. 1:7). The good news for the sinner is Jesus Christ came to earth, born of a virgin, lived a sinless life, died on a cross for the sins of the world, rose from the dead, and offers eternal live to those who will believe. This is God's grace (Isa. 53; John 3:16; Rom. 3:23; 6:23; 5:8; 10:9–10).

The Gospel of God and of Christ and of grace are the same. Paul describes this gospel as the Gospel of the grace of God to which he was totally sold out: "None of these things move me, neither count I my life dear unto myself, so that I might finish my course with joy, and the ministry, which I have received of the Lord Jesus, to testify the gospel of the grace of God" (Acts 20:24). Paul was not ashamed of the gospel of Christ: "for it is the power of God unto salvation to everyone that believeth; to the Jew first, and also to the Greek, For in it is the righteousness of God revealed from faith to faith; as it is written, the just shall live by faith" (Rom. 1:16).

The gospel of the kingdom ceased being preached when Jesus was rejected and crucified. The gospel of grace began to be preached at

Pentecost, and it will be proclaimed throughout the Church age but will cease at the end of the Church age. No one knows when this will occur. However, we do know when the Church is removed from this earth and the Holy Spirit ceases to hinder, iniquity will abound (2 Thess. 2:7). At that time, the gospel of grace will be replaced with the gospel of the kingdom preached by the Jews during the tribulation.

VI. The Everlasting Gospel is remarkably rememberable. It is the last chance for so many. It will be proclaimed shortly before the return of Jesus Christ as Lord of lords and King of kings. The message is *turn or burn*. Almost no one will believe the gospel of grace at the end of the Church age. Most will not believe the gospel of the kingdom the second time, just as most would not believe Jesus, as He walked among them. The world will lay in ruins after the plagues, war, and devastation of the tribulation. Yet, God will offer the people a last chance to repent. That offer is the everlasting Gospel to be preached by an angel:

> "And I saw another angel fly in the midst of heaven, having the everlasting gospel to preach unto them that dwell on the earth, and to every nation, and kindred, and tongue, and people, Saying with a loud voice, Fear God, and give glory to him for the hour of his judgement is come; and worship him that made heaven and earth and the sea and the fountains of waters." (Rev. 14:6–7)

This is good news for those who will turn to Jesus but very bad news for those who worship the beast (Rev. 7:9; 14:9–12).

VII. What Did Paul Mean When He Said My Gospel? In Romans 2:16 Paul speaks of a day of judgment: "In the day when God shall judge the secrets of men by Jesus Christ *according to my gospel*." Paul was speaking of judgment that all mankind will experience, either as a saved sinner or a lost person. All sin was judged on the cross. Therefore, the judgment of the individual will be directed toward their works. In 1 Corinthians 3:11–15, Paul speaks of the works of a believer and in order for those works to stand, they must be built on the foundation of Christ. Those that are not done through the power of the Holy Spirit to honor God will be burned away as hay and stubble. The works that are done to the glory of the Lord Jesus, though tried by the fire of judgment, will come out as gold, silver, and precious stone. That is why Paul said "If any man's work shall be burned, he shall suffer loss; but he himself shall be saved, yet as by fire" (1 Cor. 3:15).

For the unbeliever, they will be judged according to their works. Their judgment is the great white throne judgment.

> "And I saw the dead, small and great, stand before God, and the books were opened; and another book was opened which is the book of life. And the dead were judged out of those things which were written in the books according to their works." And the sea gave up the dead that were in it, and death and hades delivered up the dead that were in them; and they were judged every man according to their works. (Rev. 20:11–13)

So, what did Paul mean by my Gospel? Remember, Paul was preaching the Gospel of grace as he went throughout Judea, Asia Minor, Greece, Spain, and Rome. As he established churches in those places, he would either revisit the fledgling churches or write letters to the congregations. The letters could contain praise, prayer, admonishments, and even warnings. Paul was preaching and teaching the Gospel of grace in doctrine and duty and by example. These letters were to the point and would be used to govern church conduct and behavior. Even today, the full development of the Gospel of grace came through these letters of Paul. The letters are Paul's gospel.

VIII. Another Gospel; Not another but a perversion of the gospel of grace: Departing from the truth was not foreign then, and it is not foreign now. Jesus warned of false teachings. "Beware of false prophets, who come to you in sheep's clothing but inwardly they are ravening wolves. Ye shall know them by their fruits. Do men gather grapes of thorns, or figs of thistles?" (Matt. 7:15–16). Paul warned of false teachers and those who would so quickly believe a lie: "I marvel that ye are so soon removed from him that called you into the grace of Christ unto another gospel, Which is not another; but there are some that trouble you and would pervert the gospel of Christ" (Gal. 1:6–7). Paul twice says that if any man or angel preach any other gospel, let him be accursed. (Gal. 1:8–9). Paul encouraged Timothy to "keep that which is committed to thy trust, avoiding profane and vain babblings, and oppositions of *science* falsely so called. Finally, Peter warned of false teachers: "But there were false prophets also among the people, even as there shall be false teachers among you, who secretly shall bring in destructive heresies, even denying the Lord that bought them and bring upon themselves swift destruction" (2 Pet. 2:1).

Jesus and the apostles warned of another gospel and those who would spread them. Many churches of today, which embrace a social agenda that embraces so-called, false science and perverts the truth of the gospel of grace, are following in the very footsteps of those before them that Jesus condemned.

Summary: The good news given to Abram and King David is not a mystery. The gospel according to Matthew, Mark, Luke and John is not a mystery. So, what is the mystery of the gospel? The mystery is: *"The gospel is dispensationally promised, delivered, and discerned. It is promised to all. It was delivered by John the Baptist, Jesus, and His disciples. It is being delivered by the Church. It will be delivered by the 144,000 Jews, and it will be delivered by an angel. It is and will be discerned by those who believe."*

Chapter 7

Mystery of the Faith

1 Timothy 3:9

I. **Context: (1 Tim. 3:1–16)**

   ➤ Faith, the foundation of service for a bishop and deacon.
   ➤ Faith before godliness.

II. **What Is Biblical Faith? (Definition)**

   ➤ Substance, hope, and evidence (Heb. 11:1–2).
   ➤ Understanding. (Heb. 11:3).

III. **The Substance of Biblical Faith: (Substance or Foundation is what things are made of (Heb. 11:1).**

   ➤ The beginning; the author and finisher of the believer's faith (Heb. 12:2).
   ➤ How the believer receives faith (Rom. 10:17).
   ➤ The focus of faith: Father, Son, Holy Spirit (John 14:1- 26).
   ➤ The footprints of saving faith

      1. Justification by faith (Rom. 4:25; 2 Cor. 5:21; Isa. 53:10).
      2. Leads to salvation (Rom. 10:10).

3. Sanctification by faith (Acts 26:15–18; Rom. 15:16).
4. Purification by faith (1 John 1:8–9).

IV. The Things Hoped for: Biblical Hope = The Happy Anticipation of Good.

➤ Earthly anticipation:

1. The hope of the Gospel; fulfillment of all the promises contained therein (Col. 1:23).
2. The hope of righteousness (Gal. 1:6; 5:4–5).
3. The hope of salvation (1 Thess. 5:8–11).
4. The hope of God's calling (Eph. 1:17–18; 4:3–4).
5. Full assurance of hope unto the end (Heb. 6:11; 12:1; 2 Tim. 4:7–8).

➤ Heavenly anticipation:

1. The hope of the resurrections (Acts 23:6, 1 Thess. 4:16).
2. The blessed hope and appearing of the Glory of our great God and Savior Jesus Christ (Titus 2:13).
3. The hope of eternal life (Titus 1:2; 3:7).

V. The Evidence of Walking by Faith and not by sight: (2 Cor. 5:7)

➤ The believer's walk and behavior before God:

1. In newness of life starting with baptism (Rom. 6:4).
2. In Jesus (Col. 2:6–7).
3. Worthy of God (1 Thess. 2:12).
4. After the Spirit and in the Spirit (Rom. 8:1, Gal. 5:16,25).

➢ The believer's walk before other believers:

1. In love (Eph. 5:1–2; 2 John 6).
2. In light (Eph. 5:8; 1 John 1:6–7).

➢ The believer's walk before the unbeliever:

1. In wisdom (Col. 4:5–6).
2. Honesty (1 Thess. 4:12).
3. In Truth (3 John 4).

VI. What Walking by Faith Produces

➢ Fruit of the Spirit (Eph. 5:8–9).
➢ Power (Matt. 17:20).
➢ Strength and patience in trials (2 Thess. 1:4).
➢ Ability to overcome the world (1 John 5:4).

VII. Understanding the Mystery of Biblical faith: It is a journey not an Event.

The Mystery of the Faith
1 Timothy 3:9

I. Context: In 1 Timothy 3, Paul presents to Timothy two mysteries as he sets forth the qualifications of elders and deacons. The first is the mystery of the faith in verse 9, and the second is the mystery of godliness in verse 16. Without faith in the Lord Jesus Christ, there can be no godliness demonstrated by mankind. Without faith, mankind cannot please God. "But without faith it is impossible to please him; for he that cometh to God must believe that he is, and that he is a rewarder of them that diligently seek him" (Heb. 11:6). Over the centuries, many have attempted self-justification by their works. Many will go out into eternity, hoping the good works they have done here on earth will outweigh the bad deeds they committed. That kind of hope will land the person in the lake of fire. There is nothing mankind can do to save himself, and without salvation by grace through faith in the Lord Jesus, all works are useless. "For by grace are ye saved through faith; and that not of yourselves, it is the gift of God not of works, least any man should boast" (Eph. 2:8–9). The order that God has set forth for mankind is first, faith in the Lord Jesus Christ; second, godlikeness by following the example of Jesus in obedience; and third, service that honors God. "For we are his workmanship. Created in Christ Jesus unto good words, which God hath before ordained that we should walk in them" (Eph. 2:10).

II. What Is Biblical Faith? There is no need to seek a definition of faith provided by academia, for God through the writer of Hebrews has provided His definition. "Now faith is the substance of things hoped for, the evidence of things not seen" (Heb. 11:1). God defined faith, God exemplified faith through the elders of Israel (Heb. 11), and God positioned the believer to understand that not all things that are very important, are seen by the eye of man. Only faith can lead a person to accept the fact that creation was framed by God speaking it into existence. "For by it the elders received witness. Through faith, we understand that the worlds were framed by the word of God, so that things which are seen were not made of things which do appear" (Heb. 11:2–3).

According to God's Word, faith is described by three components. The first component is its substance, which is the foundation. What is the foundation of faith, and where does it come from? The second component of faith is hope that is anchored in the foundation. What is the hope of the believer? The third component is the evidence that supports its existence. What is that evidence? How does faith lead to the understanding of God's will and purpose for the believer?

III. The Substance or Foundation of Biblical Faith:

Jesus is the author and finisher of our faith: Substance refers to what faith is made of. Part of understanding what something is made of is to understand its origin. In Hebrews 12:2, the Word of God indicates that the origin of our faith is the Lord Jesus Christ. "Looking unto Jesus, the author and finisher of our faith, who for the joy that was set before him endured the cross, despising the shame, and is set down at the right hand of the throne of God." It is difficult if not impossible for the believer to understand the faith of Jesus as He hung there on the cross. Although fully God, He was fully man and was even tempted as we are (Heb. 4:15), yet, was without sin. The human side of Jesus had the ultimate faith in His own resurrection from the dead, His ascension back into heaven and the Trinity's work to redeem mankind. God the Son is all knowing, all powerful, and ever-present and knew what He would endure on the cross before the foundations of the world. However, that does not dismiss His great faith, being fully man, as He hung on the cross when He said, "It is finished." (John 19:30). Jesus is the author before creation, and finisher on the cross of our faith.

The greatest contrast of faith is that of Jesus and Satan. Satan, in a position to see the substance and evidence of the glory, majesty, and power of God, thought he could be like the Most High. He coveted the position of God. He has lied, murdered, and committed the highest sin of idolatry against God. As Jesus is the Author and Finisher of our faith, Satan is the author of sin, sin that Satan started and God will finish. As Jesus had the ultimate faith, Satan had no faith and continues to rebel as though he could possibly succeed in the end.

How the believer receives faith: As Jesus authored and finished our faith with His death on the cross, He gives all of mankind the privilege of coming to Him and accepting Him by faith as Lord and Savior. The privilege is made manifest to the lost by hearing the gospel.

"So, then, faith cometh by hearing, and hearing by the word of God" (Rom. 10:17). In the parable of the builders, Luke 6:47–49, Jesus said, "Whosoever cometh to me, and heareth my sayings, and doeth them, I will shew you to whom he is like." The one who hears and builds on faith in Jesus, the rock, is born again and lives. The one who hears and rejects Jesus and builds on the things of this world, the sand, remains spiritually dead, resulting in eternal damnation.

The focus of faith: Jesus taught His disciples to focus on their relationship to Him and His relationship to the Father while looking for the coming of the Holy Spirit into their lives. In John 14:19–20, Jesus said, "Yet a little while, and the world seeth me no more; but ye see me because I live, ye shall live also. At that day ye shall know that I am in my Father, and ye in me, and I in you." Jesus told the disciples that saving faith is grounded in Him as He indwells us through the power of the Holy Spirit. Jesus confirmed the strengthening of a believer's faith when He told the disciples, "But the Comforter, which is the Holy Spirit, whom the Father will send in my name, he shall teach you all things, and bring all things to your remembrance, whatsoever I have said unto you" (John 14:26).

The footprints of faith: Jesus made the *first footprint of faith (justification).* That step was toward the redemption of mankind. It was Jesus "Who was delivered for our offenses, and was raised again for our *justification*" (Rom. 4:25). "For he hath made him, who knew no sin, to be sin for us, that we might be made the righteousness of God in him" (2 Cor. 5:21). The author and finisher of our faith completed the first step to justify mankind before the Father by enduring the cross. Sinful man caused the suffering and pain of the prints in His nail-scarred hands and feet. Justification of the sinner comes only by and through the sacrifice of the Lord Jesus Christ on the cross of Calvary (Isa. 53:10). The footprint of the cross of Calvary is eternal.

The *second footprint of faith is salvation* determined by the individual sinner. God gave mankind a free will, and only the sinner can decide to turn to Jesus in faith. Saving faith leads to salvation, which is deliverance by God from the penalty of sin made possible only by the sacrificial death of Jesus on the cross. "For with the heart man believeth unto righteousness; and with the mouth confession is made unto salvation" (Rom. 10:10). Just as the scripture says of Abraham, "Abraham believed God, and it was counted unto him as righteousness (Rom. 4:3), the believing sinner is justified before God and is therefore pronounced and treated as righteous, making salvation by grace through faith in Jesus possible.

The *third footprint of faith is sanctification.* Being justified by Christ and receiving salvation by faith, the believer is then positioned to be sanctified by the Holy Spirit. Paul said in Romans 15:16, "That I should be the minister of Jesus Christ to the Gentiles, ministering the gospel of God that the offering up of the Gentiles might be acceptable, being sanctified by the Holy Spirit." Sanctification or to be sanctified means to be separated or set apart for a specific purpose. Paul was set apart as the apostle to the Gentiles (Acts 26:15–18).

There are two parts to sanctification. First, the believer is to separate from evil ways and evil things. "For this is the will of God, even your sanctification, that ye should abstain from fornication" (1 Thess. 4:3). Also, in Paul's second letter to Timothy, "Nevertheless, the foundation of God standeth sure, having this seal, The Lord knoweth them that are his; and, Let everyone that nameth the name of Christ depart from iniquity... If a man, therefore purge himself from these, he shall be a vessel unto honor, sanctified, and fit for the master's use, and prepared unto every good work." (2 Tim. 2:19, 21).

The second part of sanctification is to be separated unto the will and purpose of God. When the believer is separated from evil, he is positioned to be a fit vessel for God to use. Saul was a zealous legalist, believing obeying the Law would justify him. His struggle did not seem to be the evil ways and evil things of this world. Yet, he was not a fit vessel until he met Jesus and was saved. At that point of surrender in his life, Jesus sanctified him as an apostle to carry the gospel to the Gentiles. Many, as I did, after receiving Jesus as Lord and Savior, seek to know what God's will is for their lives. Knowledge of both the separation from evil and the separation unto the will of God comes from God's Word. Jesus is our High Priest and our intercessor and as He prayed for his disciples, He now intercedes for us in the same way. "Sanctify them through thy truth thy word is truth" (John 17:17). To know and understand the will of God, the believer must study His Word. There is no substitute! That is why Paul told Timothy to, "Study to show thyself approved unto God, a workman that needeth not to be ashamed, rightly dividing the word of truth" (2 Tim. 2:15).

The *fourth print of faith comes through purification.* Because the believer will live with his sin nature until the day of death, purification by faith is a continual process. The flesh continually struggles with the spirit of the believer. It is a constant warfare, and all believers are subject to sin on any given day. However, thank God for His love and provision. In 1 John 1:8–9, the warning and provision is given to the believer. "If we say that we have no sin, we deceive ourselves, and the truth is not in us. If we confess our sins, he is faithful and just to forgive us our sins, and to cleanse us from all unrighteousness."

IV. The Things Hoped for:

Earthly Anticipation: The *"hope of the gospel"* that Paul speaks of in Colossians 1:23 is the hope of the believer toward the anticipation of the fulfillment of all the promises contained in the Gospel. Paul emphasizes that with hope and the continuation in the faith, the believer would be grounded and settled and not tossed to and fro from every wind of doctrine (Eph. 4:14).

As the Galatians were embracing the law as their vehicle of justification, Paul told them, "I marvel that ye are so soon removed from him that called you into the grace of Christ unto another gospel" (Gal. 1:6) and tells them that whoever believes the law justifies them has fallen from grace. Paul warned the Galatians that *"the hope of being righteous"* before God is only by faith in Jesus Christ (Gal. 5:4–5), and the Law made no contribution to the righteousness of mankind. The believers at Galatia were not grounded and settled in the faith. Their anticipation of good had moved from grace to the law where there was no hope.

In Pauls' letter to the church at Thessalonica, he addressed the issue of how the believer should walk in anticipation of the coming of the Day of the Lord. He encourages them to comfort one another and to be sober and put on the helmet of *"the hope of salvation"* (1 Thess. 5:8–11). Paul was continually reinforcing the hope the believer has against the battles of doubt that confront them. It is no different for the individual believer today. Therefore, we must always go back to God's Word for strength and structure. He justified us by His sacrifice on the Cross. The believer is treated as righteous because of faith in what Jesus did making salvation by grace through faith in Jesus complete.

Hope of the promises of the Gospel, including justification and salvation, must be grounded before God's calling for the believer's service can be fully realized. Paul addressed the hope of the calling of the believer by the Lord to specific service in Ephesians 1:17–18 and 4:4. When God calls the believer to service, He always equips the believer for the service with spiritual gifts to be used to render the service. In fact, in Eph. 1:17, Paul is praying for God to give wisdom and knowledge to the believers at Ephesus. These are spiritual gifts.

As Paul is speaking of the *"hope of your calling"* in Ephesians 4:4, he is addressing the walk of the believer in the vocation that they have been called into. The believer must not separate God's calling to service from the vocation in which they make their livelihood. The two must be in unity for Christian service to be effective (Eph. 4:3).

Finally, as believers, we must be like the long-distance runner who is running a marathon. We must finish the race. As we run the race of life, spiritual maturity should not be static. The runner must not stop. In Hebrews 6:11, God's Word says: "And we desire that every one of you do show the same diligence to the full assurance of *hope unto the end*." Hope unto the end was demonstrated by Paul toward the end of his life when he wrote to Timothy saying, "I have fought a good fight, I have finished my course, I have kept the faith; Henceforth there is laid up for me a crown of righteousness which the Lord, the righteous judge, shall give me at that day; and not to me only, but unto all them also that love his appearing" (2 Tim. 4:7–8). The writer of Hebrews encouraged the believer to lay aside any thing that hindered and run with patience the race that is set before us. Run with patience, and run well, for many are watching (Heb. 12:1).

Heavenly anticipation: When Paul was seized in the temple for allegedly bringing Greeks into the temple and preaching the Gospel, he was rescued and bound by Roman soldiers. When it was learned he was a Roman citizen, the chief captain loosed Paul's bonds and commanded the chief priests and all the council to appear, and brought Paul down and set him before them to determine the reason for the disruption (Acts 21:27, 22:30). While addressing the Sanhedrin, Paul perceived that part of the group were Pharisees and therefore appealed to them. Paul took this tactic because the Pharisees believed in a bodily resurrection, whereas the Sadducees did not. Paul said "I am a Pharisee, the son of a Pharisee; of *"the hope and resurrection"* of the dead I am called in question (Acts 23:6). Paul indeed preached, taught, and defended the doctrine of the resurrection. Paul remained steadfast as to the truth of the resurrection and its significance to the Christian faith. Indeed, the hope of the resurrection for the believer is to anticipate meeting Jesus in a glorified body after experiencing death (1 Thess. 4:16).

A second heavenly anticipation is; *"Looking for that blessed hope, and glorious appearing of the great God and our savior Jesus Christ"* (Titus 2:13). When Paul wrote to Titus concerning church order and believer conduct, he told Titus to speak the things which become sound doctrine. The inclusion of the blessed hope of seeing our Lord and Savior Jesus Christ in all of His glory was one of the fundamental doctrines of God's Word. The believer can anticipate but cannot fathom the appearance of the Lord Jesus. We are given a glimpse of that hope by the reaction of Peter, James, and John when they were with Jesus on the Mount of Transfiguration (Matt. 17).

A third heavenly anticipation is the hope of eternal life. Again, in the letter to Titus, Paul speaks of *"In hope of eternal life,* which God, who cannot lie, promised before the world began" (Titus 1:2). Then in Titus 3:7, Paul tells Titus, "That being justified by his grace, we should be made heirs according to the hope of eternal life." The mystery of faith comes to a crescendo with the promise of being heirs and joint heirs with Christ in an eternal state that never ends. The greatest of all hope for believers is spending eternity with their Creator, Savior, Redeemer, Provider, and Sustainer.

V. The Evidence of Walking by Faith and Not by Sight (2 Cor. 5:7). In Paul's second letter to the Corinthians, he speaks of the tabernacle of the body, and if the body were dissolved (died), the believer still has the assurance by the Holy Spirit of a resurrected body. The believer has the earnest of the Spirit, the down payment, and while we are still in the earthly body; "we walk by faith, not by sight." In that walk, we labor that, whether present or absent from the body, we please God. Paul is encouraging the believers at Corinth to walk by faith as they live each day and produce works that are deemed by God to be gold, silver, and precious stones. Works that will stand up to the fiery judgement of God is what Paul is referencing (1 Cor. 3:11–15). The evidence of a godly walk by faith is demonstrated in three ways. First is the believer's behavior before God. Second is the believer's behavior before other believers, and third is the believer's behavior before the unbeliever. The writer of Hebrews echoes what Paul was saying in Hebrews 12:1: "Wherefore, seeing we also are compassed about with so great a cloud of witnesses, let us lay aside every weight, and the sin which doth so easily beset us, and let us run with patience the race that is set before us." A life dedicated to obedience and service to the Lord is evidence of commitment, but the motivation, the indwelling Holy Spirit, is not seen.

The evidence of things not seen is further explained in Hebrews 11:3; "Through faith we understand that the worlds were framed by the word of God, so that things which are seen were not made of things which do appear." We see the world around us, but not the Creator or the work of the creation.

The believers walk before God: The believer's walk before God will set the stage for the success of all other walks in life. That walk starts when a person is saved and follows Christ in baptism: "Therefore, we are buried with him by baptism into death, that as Christ was raised up from the dead by the glory of the Father, even so we also should *walk in newness of life*" (Rom. 6:4). Baptism is in complete obedience to the Word of God. It shows the world that the believer is declaring Jesus is their Lord and Savior, and their commitment is to live a life, "the newness of life," that is in obedience to God's Word.

When a person is saved and begins to walk in newness of life, with the first step displayed by being baptized, they are then to walk in Jesus. In Colossians 2:6, Paul instructs the Colossians *"As ye have, therefore, received Christ Jesus the Lord, so walk ye in him."* Paul is telling them you have started now continue in Christ. Paul is telling these believers the danger of deceitful enticing words by those who would teach heresy and to be able to sort through such lies. The believer must be "Rooted and built up in him, and established in the faith, as ye have been taught, abounding with thanksgiving" (Col. 2:7). The evidence is seen by the world but what the believer is rooted in ("Christ in you the hope of glory") is not seen (Col. 1:27).

Paul tells the believers at Thessalonica; "That ye would *walk worthy of God,* who hath called you unto his kingdom and glory" (1 Thess. 2:12). These are the words Paul had preached and was reminding the Thessalonians how he; Silas, and Timothy came and, without flattering words or financial support from them, had imparted unto them the gospel of God. The evangelistic approach of Paul, Silas, and Timothy was gentle, like a nurse toward a child. They had been role models to these new believers, and now Paul was thanking God for the response of these new believers to the Gospel they had preached to them. All believers are called to walk worthy of God. He is our Father; we are in His family, and as Christians, we should act like it. Evidence of godliness is manifest to the world that the believer is different, but his spiritual family is not seen.

In both epistles to the Romans and the Galatians, Paul instructs the believer in how to be set apart to God. He explains to the congregations in Galatia that the key to sanctification is the indwelling Holy Spirit. In Galatians 5, Paul is reinforcing his message from his previous missionary journeys that sanctification comes from the work of the Holy Spirit not the law. In Galatians 5:16, Paul told the churches, "This I say then, *Walk in the Spirit,* and ye shall not fulfill the lust of the flesh." Paul puts this in the context of attempting to please God by obeying the Law. Paul tells them; "But if ye be led by the Spirit, ye are not under the law" (Gal. 6:18). Paul tells the Galatians that a Christian's character is produced by the work of the Holy Spirit, not by the works of the flesh. Paul said in Galatians 5:25; "If we live in the Spirit, let us also walk in the Spirit." Paul spells out the result of the believer walking in the Spirit in Romans 8:1; "There is, therefore, now no condemnation to them who are in Christ Jesus, who walk not after the flesh, but after the Spirit.

The Believer's Walk Before Other Believers: In Ephesians 5:1–2, Paul reminds believers how they are to treat one another; "Be ye, therefore, followers of God, as dear children; And *walk in love,* as Christ also hath loved us, and hath given himself for us an offering and a sacrifice to God for a sweet-smelling savor." John also reminds believers how they are to act toward each other in 2 John 6: "And this is love, that we walk after his commandments. This is the commandment, that, as ye have heard from the beginning, ye should walk in it." John remembered what Jesus had told him and the other disciples when He said; "This is my commandment that ye love one another, as I have loved you" (John15:12). Paul expounds on the believers' love for each other in 1 Corinthians 13 and places love for fellow believers at the top of the list in exercising the spiritual gifts within the church body. Godly love is evidence of the indwelling Holy Spirit that cannot be seen.

Both Paul and John provide a picture of darkness and light as they relate to the believers' walk in life. In Ephesians 5:8 Paul tells the Church; "For ye were once darkness but now are ye light in the Lord; *walk as children of light.*" As John was speaking of the believers' fellowship with the Father and the Son as well as each other, he sets the condition of "If we say that we have fellowship with him, and walk in darkness, we lie and do not the truth; But if we *walk in the light,* as he is in the light, we have fellowship one with another, and the blood of Jesus Christ, his Son, cleanseth us from all sin" (1 John 1:6–7). Both John and Paul had learned the contrast from Jesus. Jesus told his disciples in Matthew 5:13–16 that they were the light of the world, and they should let their light shine for the world to see their good works that God would be glorified. That walk, that instruction, has not changed for the believer. It is just as pertinent today as it was then. So, the believer is to show evidence that the world will not understand.

The Believer's Walk Before the Unbeliever: The character of the believer is always under scrutiny by the world. How many times have you heard the statement that the church is full of hypocrites, or he or she claims to be a Christian, but they do not like it and I am as good as anyone going to that church. For the believer to be an effective witness to the unbeliever, they must realize they are being watched and measured by the world, and given the opportunity, the world will hold up the sins of a Christian to justify their own behavior.

In the context of watching what a person says, Paul said in Colossians 4:5–6; "*Walk in wisdom* toward them that are outside, redeeming the time." Paul tells them to "Let your speech be always with grace, seasoned with salt, that ye may know how ye ought to answer every man." Godly wisdom is limited to only the believer. "The fear of the LORD is the beginning of wisdom, and the knowledge of the Holy one is understanding" (Prov. 9:10). The control of the tongue is evidence of faith, but the source is not seen. James 3 provides a test for the reality of faith by a person's ability to control the tongue. That ability comes from Godly wisdom and in verse 17, the source is given: "But the wisdom that is from above is first pure, then peaceable, gentle, and easy to be entreated, full of mercy and good fruits, without partiality and without hypocrisy." Again, that kind of evidence is seen but the source is not.

Paul tells the believers at Thessalonica to be honest in their dealings with the unbeliever. "That ye may *walk honestly* toward them that are outside and that ye may have lack of nothing" (1 Thess. 4:12). Paul reminds the believers at Philippi to be "blameless and harmless, children of God without rebuke, in the midst of a crooked and perverse nation, among whom ye shine as lights in the world" (Phil. 2:15). Today we live in a crooked and perverse nation, and if the believer's light is dimmed, the world will become much darker. The evidence of honesty has dimmed greatly in the last few years in business, in politics, and in religion. The honest politician is an anomaly. Businesses operate for profit only with no regard for truth as indicated by Delta Airlines and Coca-Cola in their position on Georgia voting laws. So-called Christian religion embraces abortion, gay marriage, and many of the activities listed in the iniquity of the Amorites. The evidence of the light of honesty shines, but the source of the power is not seen.

Lying has become the norm for so many today. There is fact check, that ranks how bad a misrepresentation or lie may be on a scale of 1–5 Pinocchio's, and the politician's statement "we are doing this for the American people", ranks a 5. Some of the motives behind the lies and deception are greed and power. God hates a lying tongue (Prov. 6:17), and the believer to be credible to a lost world must speak the truth, not a person's truth as advocated by so many on the left, but the truth as measured by God's Word. John was joyful when he heard how so many of those, he had pastored behaved and said, "I have no greater joy than to hear that my children *walk in truth*" (3 John:4). John had an experience that would codify his expression of truth. In John 18:28–38, the record of the conversation between Pilate and Jesus shows such a contrast. As the Way the Truth and the Life stood before Pilate, all Pilate could say was "What is truth?" A truthful Christian is evidence of light to the unbeliever who does not understand the source.

VI. What the Walk by Faith Produces: There are four significant out-comes produced when a believer walks by faith. The first is the fruit of the spirit. In Ephesians 5:8–9, "For ye were once darkness, but now are ye light in the Lord; walk as children of light (For the *fruit of the Spirit* is in all goodness and righteousness and truth)." The second out-come produced by walking in faith is *power.* In Matthew 17:20, Jesus told His disciples that "If ye have faith as a grain of mustard seed, ye shall say unto this mountain, Move from here to yonder place; and it shall move and nothing shall be impossible unto you." The third out-come that walking by faith will produce is strength and patience in times of trial. Paul commends the believers at Thessalonica: "So that we ourselves glory in you in the churches of God for your *patience and faith* in all your persecutions and tribulations that ye endure" (2 Thess. 1:4). Also, James tells his fellow believers; "My brethren, count it all joy when ye fall into various trials, Knowing this, that the testing of your *faith worketh patience.*" Last, John encourages the believer as he is confronted with the evil of this world: "For whatever is born of God *overcometh the world;* and this is the victory that overcometh the world, even our faith" (1 John 5:4)

VII. Understanding the Mystery of Biblical Faith: Given the founda-tion (substance) of faith, the hope of faith and the evidence of faith clearly defined in the scriptures, how does the believer hold the mys-tery of the faith in a pure conscience? Biblical faith can abound or be throttled back. It depends on how much the believer will trust what God's Word says and is a doer of the Word and not a hearer only. First there comes saving faith, then comes living faith, maturing faith, and last of all, dying faith. When a person is saved how will they live. Some will live by faith, producing good works honoring God. Others will pro-duce worthless works and will be saved yet as by fire. Some will con-tinue to grow and mature as they learn more about the Lord through His Word. Others will be content to ease along with limited study of the Word. Some will come to the end of their life with apprehension and reticence. Others will be as Paul, "for to me to live is Christ and to die is gain." The mystery of faith it that it is a journey of life, not a single event. It grows as knowledge of the Word of God increases, and with greater knowledge and obedience to Him comes a pure conscience. It has a beginning but will never end.

Chapter 8

The Mystery of Godliness

1 Timothy 3:16

I. *Context:*

- ➢ Paul's instructions to Timothy in the selection of church leaders.
- ➢ Church leaders are the representatives of biblical truth.

II. *Jesus's life on earth defines godliness.*

- ➢ What godliness is:

  1. Conforming and responding to the principles God set forth.
  2. Obedience and righteous living demonstrated by Jesus (John 8:29; 10:17; Phil. 2:7–8).

- ➢ God was manifest in the flesh (Isa. 9:6, John 1:14, 14:9, Luke 2:11).
- ➢ Justified in the Spirit (Rom. 1:3–4; John 16:13–14).
- ➢ Jesus was seen of angels (Heb. 1:4–6; 12:2).
- ➢ Jesus preached to the nations (Matt. 28:19–20; Acts 1:8).
- ➢ The Gospel is believed on in the world (Acts 2:13,41).
- ➢ The Lord Jesus was received up into glory (Acts 1:9–11).

III. The Godliness of Christ will again restore man to having dominion over the earth.

- ➤ Innocence to separation and loss of dominion (Gen. 2:7, 22; 3:17–19, 24; Rom. 8:22–23).
- ➤ Restoration (Rev. 20:4).

IV. Godliness demonstrated by Paul and Timothy:

- ➤ Paul's lifestyle (2 Tim. 3:10–11).
- ➤ Paul's encouragement to Timothy (2 Tim. 3:14–17).

V. How should every Christian respond to Christ's example?

- ➤ The right mind (Phil. 2:5).
- ➤ Dedicated service (Rom. 12:1–2).
- ➤ Every menial action dedicated to the Lord (1Cor. 10:31; Col. 3:23).

VI. Christian conduct that exemplifies godliness to the world

- ➤ Christ's teachings concerning who should be the greatest among His disciples (Luke 9:46–48).
- ➤ Christ's teaching concerning self-exultation before others (Luke 14:7–11).
- ➤ Christ's teaching concerning being a servant rather than being served (Luke 22:24–27).
- ➤ Letters to the churches concerning practical Christian behavior:

  1. Behavior in your vocation (Eph. 4:1–3).
  2. Behavior before other believers (love; Col. 3:12–14, 1 Corinthians 8:9, Philippians 2:3).
  3. Behavior before unbelievers (expediency; 1 Cor. 10:23–33).

    4. Behavior before God (humility; James 4:10; 1 Peter 5:5).

> ➢ Defending the faith; resist, stay steadfast, contend for the faith. (Phil. 1:7, 17, 27; 1 Pet. 5:6–9, Jude 3).

VII. Summary of the Mystery of Godliness

The Mystery of Godliness
1 Timothy 3:16

I. Context: In chapter 3 of 1 Timothy, Paul is giving Timothy direction on the selection of bishops and deacons who would serve in the church. As, Paul outlines the qualifications for them and their wives, he injects another very important principle, which is the mystery of godliness. Paul uses the phrase to accentuate the principle of behavior in the church by the church leadership: "But if I tarry long, that thou mayest know how thou oughtest to behave thyself in the house of God, which is the church of the living God, the pillar and ground of the truth" (1 Tim. 3:15). Jesus said in John 14:6; "I am the way the truth and the life; no man cometh unto the Father but by me." Jesus founded the church upon Himself, the church is the body of Christ, and as Jesus is the personification of truth, so should the church represent the truth. To consistently speak the truth, especially the truth about Jesus, and the truth that the Word of God provides, a person must be saved and not be a novice when it comes to the Word of God (1 Tim. 3:6). The picture is that of a godly person in the service of the Church, the body of Christ.

II. Jesus's Life on Earth Defines Godliness. Godliness is conforming and responding to the principles that God set forth in His Word that produces obedience and righteous living as demonstrated by the Lord Jesus during His earthly ministry. Jesus said in John 8:29, "And he that sent me is with me. The Father hath not left me alone; for I do always those things that please him." Obedience of Jesus to the Father was to the death. "Therefore, doth my Father love me, because I lay down my life, that I might take it again" (John 10:17). "But made himself of no reputation, and took upon him the form of a servant, and was made in the likeness of men; And, being found in fashion as a man he humbled himself and became obedient unto death, even the death of the cross" (Phil. 2:7–8).

God the Son, in the person of the Lord Jesus Christ, came to earth to lay down his life to redeem mankind. This plan which is without controversy a great mystery: "*God was manifest in the flesh.*" God set forth His plan of redemption to bring man back to a point of being able to seek to be god like. The road to redemption for man began with the Son of God, coming in the flesh. "For unto us a child is born, unto us a son is given, and the government shall be upon his shoulder; and his name shall be called Wonderful, Counselor, The Mighty God, the Everlasting Father, The Prince of Peace" (Isa. 9:6). "And the Word was made flesh, and dwelt among us and we beheld his glory the glory as of the only begotten of the Father, full of grace and truth" (John 1:14). Jesus told Phillip, "If you have seen me, you have seen the Father" (John 14:9). The angel's announcement "For unto you is born this day in the city of David a Savior who is Christ the Lord" (Luke 2:11) brought Isaiah's prophecy to fruition. *Who would believe God came in the flesh to save man from the penalty of his sin? Only the Redeemed!*

God the Son, the Lord Jesus Christ, was *justified in the Spirit*. Jesus was deemed and declared to be righteous in the Holy Spirit. Jesus was justified *in* the Spirit and not *by* the Spirit because the Holy Spirit dwelled in Him. Paul said in Romans 1:3–4, "Concerning his Son, Jesus Christ our Lord, who was made of the seed of David according to the flesh, And declared to be the Son of God with Power, according to the spirt of holiness, by the resurrection from the dead." What was already manifest in the spiritual world was revealed to man on earth at the baptism of Jesus by John the Baptist. "And the Holy Spirit descended in a bodily shape like a dove upon him, and a voice came from heaven, which said, Thou art my beloved Son; in thee I am well pleased." Jesus was righteous and deemed to be right in the spirit, not by man or any other but by the power of the Godhead (Father, Son, and Holy Spirit). Jesus would send the Spirit of truth who would guide the believer into all truth. He would not speak of Himself but would glorify Jesus (John 16:13–14). *Who can comprehend what the Godhead (Father, Son, Holy Spirit) is doing for a lost and dying world? Only the Redeemed!*

Jesus was seen by angels. In Hebrews 1:4–6 the scripture says:

> "Being made so much better than the angels, as he hath by inheritance obtained a more excellent name than they. For unto which of the angels said he at any time, Thou art my Son, this day have I begotten thee? And again, I will be to him a Father, and he shall be to me a Son? And again, when he bringeth in the first-begotten into the world, he saith, "And let all the angels of God worship him."

The angels stood before Jesus prior to the creation, at his birth, during His life on earth and during the crucifixion, death, and resurrection. Jesus was seen then and is now seen by the angels at the right hand of God the Father. The believer is "Looking unto Jesus, the author and finisher of our faith, who for the joy that was set before him endured the cross, despising the shame, and is set down at the right hand of the throne of God" (Heb. 12:2). As the believer on earth is looking forward to seeing Jesus, the angels are already in His presence. *Only the believer can stand in awe of what God has done!*

Jesus is preached unto the nations. The instructions Jesus gave to His disciples, which includes the Church, is found in Matthew 28:19–20:

"Go ye, therefore, and teach all nations, baptizing them in the name of the Father, and of the Son, and of the Holy Spirit, Teaching them to observe all things whatsoever I have commanded you; and, lo, I am with you always, even unto the end of the Age. Amen" (So be it). After His resurrection, and before His ascension, Jesus instructed His disciples how to go to all nations preaching the gospel: "When ye shall receive power, after the Holy Spirit is come upon you; and ye shall be witnesses unto me both in Jerusalem, and in all Judea, and in Samaria, and unto the uttermost part of the earth." (Acts 1:8). This was the blueprint the early church was forced to use. The progression came about because of persecution. First in Jerusalem, then it followed those who carried the gospel as demonstrated by the persecution of the church. Saul of Tarsus was one of the chief persecutors in Jerusalem and Judea. But, when he was confronted by Jesus on his way to Damascus, Saul became Paul, and the gospel went to many Gentile nations. The three missionary journeys of Paul started to evangelize the whole known world. The gospel is still being preached throughout the world, and many are still being saved. However, the world is still in the persecution mode, and it will continue until the Lord Jesus comes back. *Only the believer can understand this. To a lost world it is a mystery!*

The gospel of the Lord Jesus Christ is believed on in the world. The commission by the Lord Jesus to His disciples and the results were eye-opening to the world, first at Pentecost. As many turned to Jesus and were saved, others mocked (Acts 2:13, 41). From the time of Pentecost until now, the same pattern of receiving salvation by grace through faith in the Lord Jesus Christ has not changed. Some are saved while some mock. *Those who mock do not understand the mystery and do not believe their continued rejection of the Lord Jesus and their mockery of those who do accept Him will doom them to hell.*

The Lord Jesus was received up into glory. Yes, Jesus did ascend up into glory! "And, when he had spoken these things, while they beheld, he was taken up, and a cloud received him out of their sight" (Acts 1:9). As the Lord's disciples are looking steadfastly toward heaven, they are asked by two angels why they were gazing up into heaven? They were then told Jesus will come again in like manner (Acts 1:10–11). As the disciples were encouraged, so, is the church. We are to *go,* not *gaze!*

III. Man Again Restored to Having Dominion Over the Earth: By the obedience of Jesus Christ to the Father, mankind will again be restored. As each step of God's provision was revealed and demonstrated through the obedience of Christ, mankind again is placed in a position of being restored. Adam and Eve were created in innocence, separated from God by sin, resulting in man losing dominion over the earth (Gen. 2:7, 22; 3:17–19, 24; Rom. 8:22–23). That dominion will be restored when Jesus comes again and sets up His 1000-year reign (Rev. 20:4). At that time, most will understand the mystery of godliness because Jesus will be sitting on His throne as King of kings and Lord of lords, ruling with a rod of iron. Godliness will be first and foremost in man's mind as they witness the rule of the king.

IV. Godliness Demonstrated by Paul and Timothy: So, what does it mean for a person to be godly? The answer to the question helps unravel the mystery of godliness that Paul references. Godliness is wrapped up in and communicated through the truth of the Word of God and faith in Jesus Christ. Paul fully demonstrated a lifestyle of godliness and will tell Timothy later in 2 Timothy 3:10–11: "But thou hast fully known my doctrine, manner of life, purpose, faith, long-suffering, love, patience, persecutions, afflictions which came unto me at Antioch, at Iconium, at Lystra, what persecutions I endured; but out of them all the Lord delivered me." Paul further encourages Timothy in 2 Timothy 3:14–17:

"But continue thou, in the things which thou hast
learned and hast been assured of, knowing of whom
thou hast learned them, and that from a child thou
hast known the holy scriptures, which are able to make
thee wise unto salvation through faith which is in Christ
Jesus. All scripture is given by inspiration of God, and
is profitable for doctrine, for reproof for correction, for
instruction in righteousness, That the man of God may
be perfect, thoroughly furnished unto all good works."

Being grounded in the Word and demonstrating godliness through
action of deed is a mystery to the novice and unbeliever.

**V. How Should Every Christian Respond to Christ's Example of
Godliness?** Paul's letter to Philippian Christians was to "Let this mind be
in you, which was also in Christ Jesus" (Phil. 2:5). This was a mind-set of
obedience to God, humility and the attitude and demonstration of service to others. In Romans 12:1–2, Paul, begged the Roman Christians
to "present your bodies as living sacrifices, holy, acceptable unto God
which is your reasonable service." Everything a believer thinks or does
should reflect their walk with the Lord. One's mind and body should
be totally given over to God. The result should be whatever one does,
even menial task of life, should be done to the glory of God (1 Cor.
10:31; Col. 3:23). Christians are to please God, *not* man.

VI. Christian Conduct that Exemplifies Godliness to the World:
The teachings of Jesus to His disciples

Jesus taught his disciples a profound *lesson concerning humility* in
Luke 9:27–48. Peter John, and James had just been with Jesus during
the Lord's transfiguration and the appearance of Moses and Elijah. The
other disciples had remained behind, and as Jesus came down from
the mountain, He was met by many people. One was a father whose

son was demon possessed. The disciples could not cast out the demon, so the father begged Jesus to cast out the demon, and He did. The fact that Peter, James, and John who were with Jesus while the rest of the disciples were attempting to cast out a demon could have possibly created the conversation. As the disciples reasoned among themselves which of them should be the greatest in the kingdom, Jesus took a little child "And said unto them, Whosoever shall receive this child in my name, receiveth me; and whosoever shall receive me receiveth him that sent me; for he that is least among you all, the same shall be great" (Luke 9:48). The Greek word for receive is *dechomai*, meaning to give hospitality. In the affairs of Jewish men, a child held a very humble position. For a Jewish man to take a child who is a stranger and treat him with hospitality was not the norm. Just as the Pharisees ignored most of the common people around them, ignoring a child was the common approach. The implication is the child is not worth my time. To the Pharisee, the thought was, I am above the commoner, and I will show them contempt, not courtesy. The attitude was made obvious with the treatment of the woman who anointed Jesus's feet at the Pharisee's house and the prayer of the Pharisee versus the publican's. Both Pharisees were looking down on those they perceived to be below them (Luke 7:36–50, 18:14).

Jesus taught another lesson to His disciples concerning exalting one's self in Luke 14:7–11. Jesus was eating a meal at one of the chief Pharisee's house and was watching how the guest were choosing the best positions for their seating. Jesus uses a very practical example in a parable of a wedding feast and those who would attend in order to call out the self-exultation. Jesus told His disciples, if they were invited to a wedding feast, never take the most honored seats but take the lower seats lest you become embarrassed when the householder asks you to take a lower seat. It is better for the guest to be asked to go up to a better seat than to be asked by the host to step down to a lower seat. In a confrontation with the Pharisees, Jesus applied the same principle when He told the Pharisees, "Jesus answered, If I honor myself, my honor is nothing, it is my Father that honoreth me, of whom ye say, that he is your God" (John 8:54). Proclaiming how great one is by one's own self is not godliness. Every talent a person has is a gift from God. Every spiritual gift a person has is a gift from God. Man has no platform to brag on self. Many believe they are a legend in their own eyes.

Christ's teaching concerning being a servant rather than being served (Luke 22:24–27).

Strife again was raised among the disciples as they discussed which of them should be considered the greatest. Jesus told them "But ye shall not be so; but he that is greatest among you, let him be as the younger; and he that is chief as he that doth serve. For which is greater, he that dineth, or he that serveth? Is not he that dineth? But I am among you as he that serveth" (Luke 22:26–27). At the last Passover, Jesus demonstrated the principal when he washed the disciple's feet and instructed them: "If I, then your Lord and Master, have washed your feet, ye also ought to wash one another's feet. For I have given you an example, that ye should do as I have done to you" (John 13:14–15).

Letters to the early churches concerning practical Christian behavior

When Jesus was teaching his disciples, the church body had not been established and Paul was a devout Pharisee who hated Christians. All this changed when Jesus called out Paul on the road to Damascus, and Paul totally surrendered to the Lord. As Paul went about establishing churches in his three missionary journeys, he continued to teach the early churches how to behave before a crooked and perverse world. Paul stated to the church at Philippi: "That ye may be blameless and harmless children of God without rebuke, in the midst of a crooked and perverse nation, among whom ye shine as lights in the world," (Phil. 2:15). Paul encouraged godly behavior in four areas:

1. **Behavior in your vocation:** "I therefore, the prisoner of the Lord, beseech you that ye walk worthy of the vocation to which ye are called, with all lowliness and meekness, with long-suffering, forbearing one another in love, Endeavoring to keep the unity of the Spirit in the bond of peace" (Eph. 4:1–3). The world has little interest in the Christian's talk; the world is watching the Christian's walk.

2. **Behavior before other believers (Love of fellow believers):** The Holy Spirit led Paul to say many things to the early churches concerning love for fellow believers. Paul warned the church members at Corinth not to let their liberty (doing any legitimate act such as eating meat sacrificed to a pagan god1 Cor. 8:4) become a stumbling block to a weak believer. He said "But take heed lest by any means this liberty of yours become a stumbling block to them that are weak" (1 Cor. 8:9). Paul told the believers at Philippi "Let nothing be done through strife or vainglory, but in lowliness of mind let each esteem others better than themselves" (Phil. 2:3). To the church at Colossae Paul wrote: "Put on, therefore, as the elect of God, holy and beloved, tender mercies, kindness, humbleness of mind, meekness, longsuffering; Forbearing one another and forgiving one another, if any man have a quarrel against any; even as Christ forgave you, so also do ye. And above all these things put on love, which is the bond of perfectness" (Col. 3:12–14). Christian love for each other was further emphasized in 1 Corinthians 13. A person could have an abundance of spiritual gifts, but without love, they are nothing.

3. **Behavior before unbelievers (Expediency):** In 1 Corinthians 10:23–33 Paul gives instruction on how to act before an unbeliever. The context is that of having a meal with an unbeliever. If the meal is set before you, eat it and do not ask questions. However, if the meal was set before you, and the unbeliever says it is dedicated to his god, do not eat it. Paul said in 1 Corinthians 10:31, "Whether, therefore, ye eat, or drink or whatever ye do, do all to the glory of God." When dealing with an unbeliever, you cannot isolate yourself. Paul said if you did, you would have to get out of the world (1 Cor. 5:10. However, a believer should never compromise when the gospel is in question to the unbeliever.

4. **Behavior before God (Humility):** How is the believer to act before God? We are to be humble. God is our Creator, Redeemer, Savior, and Sustainer. We can repay nothing to God; we can only trust and obey Him and come before Him in all humility "for God resisteth the proud, and giveth grace to the humble. Humble yourselves therefore under the mighty hand of God, that he may exalt you in due time" (1 Pet. 5:5). Likewise, James said "Humble yourselves in the sight of the Lord, and he shall lift you up" (James 4:10).

Defending the faith: Jesus told his disciples several times the world would hate them: "And ye shall be hated of all men for my name's sake" (Luke 21:17). In that circumstance, how is the Christian to react? In Luke 21:19, Jesus said: "In your patience possess ye your souls." As a believer, we must not let emotions dictate behavior. In addressing the law as it applied to personal retribution, Jesus said: "And unto him that smiteth thee on the one cheek offer also the other; and him that taketh away thy cloke forbid not to take thy coat also" (Luke 6:29). Jesus is addressing an individual's desire to respond to a personal attack. When the gospel is either shared or attacked, that is totally different.

Christians are not to be despondent and passive when it comes to the gospel. In Philippians 1:17, Paul says, "I am set for the defense of the gospel," and again in verse 27, he encourages the Philippians to "stand fast in one spirit, with one mind striving together for the faith of the gospel." This is not a passive attitude, and Paul was hated and maligned for his bold sharing of the gospel. Again, Jude addresses those who would bring heresy into the church:

> "Beloved when I gave all diligence to write unto you of the common salvation, it was needful for me to write unto you, and exhort you that ye should earnestly con-tend for the faith which was once delivered unto the saints. For there are certain men crept in unawares who were before of old ordained to this condemnation, ungodly men turning the grace of our God into lasciv-iousness and denying the only Lord God and our Lord Jesus Christ." (Jude 3-4))

In these circumstances, the believer is to resist, stay steadfast, and contend for the faith.

VII. Summary: By looking at the definition and the example of god-liness as shown by the life and death of Jesus Christ and how Paul and Timothy sought to live, the mystery is now uncovered. By nature, mankind is not godly. Man's ungodliness and rebellion and God's pro-vision for redemption through the sacrifice of His son on the cross of Calvary for the sins of the world helps us understand the mystery of godliness. The god-likeness set forth by the Lord Jesus redeems man-kind from his rebellion against God. Man was created in innocence, given dominion over the earth, sinned, and as a result separated from

God. That separation will result in death and hell for the one who rejects what Jesus did to restore mankind. Godliness originated and was made visible to the world by Christ Jesus. It was understood and practiced by Paul and Timothy before the early churches and was encouraged by the church leaders for all believers. This leaves rejection of the truth a matter of spiritual life or death.

Chapter 9

The Mystery of Iniquity

2 Thessalonians 2:7 Sin = Transgression, Trespass, Iniquity

I. Context:

- ➢ Is all sin the same to God?
- ➢ Iniquity is now hindered by the Holy Spirit (2 Thess. 2:1–12).
- ➢ When the Holy Spirit is taken out of the way sin will abound.
- ➢ Iniquity results in fiery trials for the believer. (1 Pet. 4:12–19).

II. What is the meaning of Iniquity?

- ➢ Iniquity means lawlessness or wickedness. In 2 Thess. 2:3, the phrase "man of sin" (lawless one) suggests the idea of contempt of divine law.
- ➢ Lawlessness attempts the overthrow of the divine government. All restraint is removed as the Holy Spirit is withdrawn (2 Thess. 2:7).
- ➢ As iniquity comes to full bloom, those that engage in it will also enjoy it. (2 Thess. 2:12).
- ➢ Iniquity is a continuous practice, not the commitment of a single act.
- ➢ Sin is an act of disobedience to divine law, missing the mark.

1. Sin is not imputed when there is no law (Rom. 5:13).
2. I had not known sin but by the law (Rom. 7:7).
3. Without the law sin was dead (Rom. 7:8).
4. For by the law is the knowledge of sin (Rom. 3:20).

➤ Trespass is a false step, a blunder; sin in ignorance (Lev. 5:15–19, Num. 15:27–31).

➤ Transgression means to go aside. A breach of the known law. Presumptuous sins are sins committed with knowledge and deliberation and contrivance. Presumptuous sin is iniquity (Num. 15:27–31). Repeated commission of the same sin is presumptuous sin (2 Pet. 2:10).

III. When and where did iniquity originate?

➤ Satan is the originator of iniquity who sinned presumptuously, the god of this world (Ezek. 28:15; 2 Cor. 4:4).

➤ Satan will counterfeit the fullness of the godhead, divine law and government.

1. Father, Son, Holy Spirit (Col. 2:8–9).
2. Dragon, Beast out of the Sea, Beast out of the Earth (False Prophet, Rev. 13, 19:20).

IV. How has man embraced iniquity?

➤ Only accountable to self.

➤ The Liberal Progressive Ideology:

1. "According to Kartain:
2. According to Dr. J.L. Riley:

3. Iniquity attempting to overthrow divine government as well as total rejection of God's law and will by substituting the will of self.

➤ Man tries to define the boundaries of right and wrong, redefining them depending upon the circumstance, doing what is right in his own eyes.

1. Idolatry (Judg. 17:6).
2. Moral degradation (Judg. 19:1).
3. Civil war (Judg. 21:25).
4. The way of a fool is right in his own eyes (Prov. 12:15).
5. Every way of a man is right in his own eyes (Prov. 21:2).
6. Fools today are self-described as liberal progressives.

V. What is the progression of Iniquity? (James 1:14–15)

1. Temptation
2. Lust
3. Enticement
4. Lust conceived.
5. Bringing forth *sin*
6. When *sin* is finished, it brings forth death. (Rom. 6:23).

VI. The Manifestation of Iniquity:

➤ Through spiritual leadership.
➤ Through society's values. "Value Systems developed by man, leaving God out."
➤ Through government leadership.

VII. The deadly spiral and consequences of Iniquity

- ➢ All history shows nations tend to become more and more wicked.
- ➢ When iniquity gets to the point where God ceases to tolerate it, He will destroy mankind (Gen. 6:30–37), even when there is no law.
- ➢ When a culture, people, nation becomes so wicked, their iniquity is full, God will destroy them (Gen. 15:16, Josh. 10:12–27).
- ➢ Individually, man can repent; collectively nations do not!
- ➢ When the whole world's iniquity becomes full, God will destroy all civilizations (Rev. 19:11–21).

VIII. Summary of the Mystery of Iniquity

1. Conceived by Satan.
2. Believed by mankind.
3. Imputed by the law.
4. Hindered by the Holy Spirit.
5. Progressively gets worse with man's values and laws implemented.
6. Reaches its fullness when the Holy Spirit ceases to hinder.
7. Started by Satan; finished by God at the end of the 1000-year reign.

The Mystery of Iniquity
2 Thessalonians 2:7

I. Context:

We have heard many times the phrase: "Sin is Sin and there is no difference in God's eyes." Is that true? The scripture says; "For all have sinned and come short of the glory of God" (Rom. 3:23), "For the wages of sin is death, but the gift of God is eternal life through Jesus

Christ, our Lord" (Rom. 6:23) and "Whosoever committeth sin trans-gresseth also the law; for sin is the transgression of the law" (1 John 3:4). As we start to dig into what the Holy Spirit led Paul to write to the church at Thessalonica, more light is shed on the question. Paul was writing the believers at Thessalonica to comfort them concerning their perception that the day of the Lord was present (2 Thess. 2:1–12). Paul warned of the deception and clearly points to the fact there would first be a falling away of the Church and then the revealing of the man of sin, the son of perdition, the Antichrist, who will set himself up as a god. In so doing, Paul reminds these believers he had already told them of events that would take place. The man of sin was yet to be revealed because evil was still being restrained by the Holy Spirit. When the Holy Spirit who hinders and restraints are taken out of the way, the wicked one would be revealed. Paul stated to these believers as well as believers of today, "For the mystery of iniquity doth already work; only he who now hindereth will continue to hinder until he be taken out of the way" (2 Thess. 2:7) *What is meant by the short phrase, the mystery of iniquity and it doth already work?*

Peter was led by the Holy Spirit to write to fellow believers concerning the fiery trials they were experiencing in 1 Peter 4:12–19. The suffering was the result of persecution by unbelievers. These believers were already experiencing iniquity at work. They were being reproached for the name of Christ. Peter tells them to not be surprised and rejoice in that they are partakers of Christ's suffering. The same that was going on in that day is going on today. But, will it intensify and if so, how should the believer see this in the context of the mystery of iniquity? Iniquity then and iniquity now, what is the mystery?

II. What Is the Meaning of Iniquity? Iniquity and lawlessness are rendered the same in the Greek. It literally means lawlessness or wickedness. The Greek word is *anomia* (ἀνομία).[14] The man of sin referenced by Paul in 2 Thessalonians 2:7, meaning the lawless one, implies the idea of contempt for divine law. In fact, lawlessness attempts the overthrow of divine government (God the Father, Son, Holy Spirit, Man, Woman, Children, God's order) and divine law. Paul is telling the believers at Thessalonica the full bloom of iniquity will take place when the constraint of the Holy Spirit is removed. This brings us back to the question" is sin just sin and does God differentiate?

First, we must look at sin as it is laid out in the Bible. Sin can be a trespass, a transgression, and iniquity. Are there differences? Yes! Sin comes from the Greek word *hamartian* (ἁμαρτία), meaning an act of disobedience to divine law.[15] It means to miss the mark. However, sin is not imputed when there is no law (Rom. 5:13). Paul said I had not known sin but by the law (Rom. 7:7), and without the law, sin was dead (Rom. 7:8). Paul said "for by the law is the knowledge of sin (Rom. 3:20). Once the law was given, God imputed sin to man. *A trespass, a false step, or blunder, means to sin in ignorance of the Law* (Num. 15:27–31). The Greek word is *paratoma* (παράπτωμα).[16] *A transgression meaning to go aside is a breach of the known Law.* "for where no law is, there is no transgression" (Rom. 4:15). The Greek word is *parabalino* (παραβαίνω).[17] In speaking of the suffering and sacrifice of Christ (Isa. 53:8), "for the transgression of my people was he stricken."

Both the trespass sin and the transgression sin were judged by the Law. For a trespass sin, the law made provision: "And if any soul sin through ignorance, then he shall bring a she-goat of the first year for a sin offering" (Num. 15:27). To the Israelite who knew the law and

---

14   Vine, W.E. *Expository Dictionary of New Testament Words.*

15   Ibid.

16   Ibid.

17   Ibid.

disobeyed it anyway, a transgression could carry a much stiffer penalty. The act was called sinning presumptuously. "But the soul that doeth anything presumptuously, whether he is born in the land or a sojourner, the same reproacheth the LORD; and that soul shall be cut off from the people. Because he hath despised the word of the LORD, and hath broken his commandment, that soul shall utterly be cut off, his iniquity shall be upon him" (Num. 15:30–31).

The scripture provides many examples of the transgression penalty. God commanded a man to be stoned to death for picking up sticks on the sabbath day (Num. 15:32–36). "Saul died for his transgression which he committed against the LORD, even against the word of the LORD, which he kept not, and also for asking counsel of a medium to inquire of her, and inquired not of the LORD; therefore, he slew him, and turned the kingdom unto David, the son of Jesse" (1 Chron. 10:13–14). *Presumptuous sin can easily become iniquity.* It is committed with full knowledge, deliberation, and contrivance. Peter provides a description of these people: "But chiefly them that walk after the flesh in the lust of uncleanness, and despise government. Presumptuous are they; self-willed, they are not afraid to speak evil of dignities" (2 Pet. 2:10).

III. When and Where Did Iniquity Originate?

However, the sin of iniquity preceded the law. Satan was the originator of iniquity, which occurred before the creation of the world. He is also the champion of iniquity. "Thou wast perfect in thy ways from the day that thou wast created, till iniquity was found in thee" (Ezek. 28:15). The fullness of iniquity is found in Satan's desires and intent. His desire is to be like God. "I will ascend above the heights of the clouds, I will be like the Most High" (Isa. 14:14). Satan's attempt to be like the Most High is demonstrated through his intent to rule over the whole earth. Paul gives insight into this attempt in 2 Corinthians

4:4: "In whom the god of this age hath blinded the minds of them who believe not, lest the light of the glorious gospel of Christ, who is the image of God, should shine unto them."

The fullness of Satan's iniquity is manifest in his effort to counterfeit the fullness of the godhead. Paul warns of such: "Beware lest any man spoil you through philosophy and vain deceit after the tradition of men, after the rudiments of the world and not after Christ. For in him dwelleth all the fullness of the Godhead bodily" (Col. 2:8–9). As Paul is speaking of God the Father, Son, and Holy Spirit, Satan will introduce a counterfeit trinity and through deceit cause many to worship him. "And they worshiped the dragon who gave power unto the beast; and they worshiped the beast, saying, Who is like the beast? Who is able to make war with him?" (Rev. 13:4). As the dragon, (Satan), will counterfeit God the Father, he will use the beast out of the sea who is wounded to death to counterfeit God the Son in death and resurrection. As the Holy Spirit witnesses of and glorifies Jesus (John 16:14), the false prophet will witness of the beast out of the sea "and causeth the earth and them who dwell on it to worship the first beast whose deadly wound was healed" (Rev. 13:12). This is the false prophet (Rev. 19:20), completing the false trinity.

IV. How Has Man Embraced Iniquity?

We see through the scripture where the fullness of iniquity has come and where it is headed. In Genesis 6:5 we read:

> "And God saw that the wickedness of man was great in the earth, and that every imagination of the thoughts of his heart was only evil continually and it repented the LORD that he had made man on the earth, and it grieved him at his heart. And the LORD said, I will destroy man whom I have created from the face of

the earth; both man, and beast, and the creeping thing, and the fowls of the air; for it repenteth me that I have made them."

This was iniquity, without the established law. Again, in Genesis 15, Abraham is told by God of the future inheritance of the land of Canaan by his descendants. The time would be four generations hence (Gen. 15:16) and would occur when the iniquity of the Amorites was completed. God destroyed all of civilization except Noah and his family, and God destroyed the Amorites for the fullness of their iniquity.

But how has the downward spiral continued? Iniquity intensifies its downward spiral (becomes more wicked) as man seeks to be his own god, thus accountable to no one but self. This is exemplified in the efforts of man over time to rid the world of any influence of the God of creation. A great example of this is the willful king that does according to his own will (Dan. 11:36–37). He regards neither god nor anyone but only magnifies himself above all. As this very well could be Antiochus Epiphanes of the old Greek empire who sought to destroy Jewish worship by offering a sow upon the temple altar. It also identifies with the beast out of the sea. Antiochus, though insignificant in international history, gained a place in history for his treachery against the Jews. Although the iniquity of Antiochus happened hundreds of years ago, and the beast is yet to come, does man really believe he should define what is good and evil? Does man really think he can usurp authority over God's divine law and government?

What of today? Although, old news to the liberal progressive, the elimination of prayer in schools, removal of the Ten Commandments from public property, legal abortion at any time, and legally redefining marriage and gender all represent further steps to man setting himself up as a god. Three quotes from the liberal progressive movement are worth mentioning. They personify man attempting to be his own god.

1. "According to *Kartain*: "Society being composed of a plurality of persons, each with his own aims, interests, and conceptions of the good; is best arranged when it is governed by principles that do not themselves presuppose any particular conception of good."[18]

2. *Dr. J.L. Riley* states "Society is constantly changing. That which exists is not sacred or perfect. Nothing is protected by divine intervention. You produce a better world by using careful analysis through mankind's rational capabilities to shape and mold institutions, beliefs and values."[19]

3. *President Joe Biden* states "I will be the most progressive president in the history of the United States." Biden is saying; I will be the most wicked president ever to hold the office of the president of the United States.

This is the *iniquity* of man attempting to overthrow divine government as well as total rejection of God's law and will by substituting the will of self and the people. Iniquity abounds in Satan and in mankind.

Should believers today be surprised at the moral and spiritual downward spiral of the United States and the world? A student of the Word of God should not be surprised. Israel followed the pattern of rebellion, moral degradation, idolatry, judgment, repentance, and

---

[18]   Carter, Ian, "Positive and Negative Liberty" The Stanford Encyclopedia of Philosophy.

[19]   Dr. Jim L. Riley, *Moderate Political Ideologies: Liberalism and Conservatism.*

restoration throughout the times of the judges and kings of both the northern and southern kingdoms. Although revival and restoration did occur numerous times, the downward spiral of iniquity toward destruction continued.

When a nation's leadership does not regard the God of creation and sets up itself as the ultimate arbitrator of good and evil, disaster will be inevitable. This is foolishness at the highest levels. Proverbs 12:15 states: "The way of a fool is right in his own eyes," and Proverbs 21:2 states: "Every way of a man is right in his own eyes.

V. What Is the Progression of Iniquity?

Just as iniquity began with Satan and led to a revolt of a third of the angels in heaven, it begins with the individual but can easily lead to influencing a whole nation. From James 1:14–15: "But every man is tempted, when he is drawn away of his own lust, and enticed. Then when lust hath conceived, it bringeth forth sin; and sin when it is finished, bringeth forth death." As the Holy Spirit led James to state this biblical principle, many great examples come from the Old Testament show how an individual's choice leads to iniquity at a national level. One example is that of the split of the kingdom of Israel. When King Solomon died, the kingdom of Israel split into the northern kingdom ruled by King Jeroboam, the son of Nebat, and the southern kingdom, ruled by Rehoboam the son of Solomon. The worship center for all Israelites was in Jerusalem the capital of the Southern Kingdom. To discourage the citizens from the northern kingdom from going to Jerusalem to worship, Jeroboam built his own worship sites. In 1 Kings 12:25–33, a record of Jeroboam's iniquity is recorded.

"And Jeroboam said in his heart, Now, shall the kingdom return to the house of David. If this people go up to do sacrifice in the house of the LORD at Jerusalem, then shall the heart of this people turn again unto their lord, even unto Rehoboam, king of Judah, and they shall kill me, and go again to Rehoboam, king of Judah. Whereupon the king took counsel and made two calves of gold, and said unto them, It is too much for you to go up to Jerusalem; behold thy gods, O Israel, which brought thee up out of the land of Egypt." Jeroboam went on to setup places of worship at Bethel and Dan, make priests of the lowest of the people who were not Levites, establish feasts and sacrifices to the calves. All this was "devised in his own heart" (1 Kings 12:13).

Jeroboam was *tempted* to change the whole structure of worship that God had ordained through the Levitical system. He was drawn to the *lust* for power and *enticement* of position by making the change. The iniquity was *conceived* and devised in his own heart, and the plan brought forth *sin*. The sin brought forth the death of the northern kingdom 210 years later. For Jeroboam's gross iniquity, God judged him by cutting off every male of his family. (1 Kings 14:9–10).

Iniquity starts at an individual level but can permeate society, and when it reaches critical mass, can destroy a whole nation. What is the leadership of this nation and others doing now that will lead to sin and death?

VI. What Is the Manifestation of Iniquity?

Iniquity is increased and made more obvious when spiritual, social, and government leadership ignores God's truth and goes about to "establish their own truth." The northern kingdom (Ephraim) was the first to go into captivity under the Assyrians for their wickedness. Spiritual leadership was void. The kings were wicked, as demonstrated by Jeroboam, the son of Nebat who drove Israel from following the LORD, and made them sin a great sin (2 Kings 17:20–23). Hosea summed it up in Hosea 9:7–9:

> "The days of judgement are come, the days of recompense are come; Israel shall know it; the prophet is a fool, the spiritual man is mad, for the *multitude of thine iniquity*, and the great hatred. The watchman of Ephraim was with my God; but the prophet is a snare of a fowler in all his ways, and hatred in the house of his God. They have deeply corrupted themselves, as in the days of Gibeah; therefore, he will remember their iniquity, he will judge their sins."

The iniquity of the men of Gibeah was sodomy and homosexual behavior (Judg. 19:14–30). In 721 BC, Assyria captured the northern kingdom of Israel and removed the captives from the land (2 Kings 17:6).

As God's judgment fell upon the northern kingdom, so did it later fall upon the southern kingdom. As the destruction of Jerusalem by the Babylonians loomed over the southern kingdom, Jeremiah warned the people that unless they repented of their sins, their city would be destroyed. It was destroyed in 586 BC. Jeremiah was the only spiritual leader speaking out concerning the coming destruction. "For from the least of them even unto the greatest of them every one is given to covetousness; and from the prophet even unto the priest every one dealeth falsely. They have healed also the hurt of the daughter of my people slightly, saying, Peace, peace; when there is no peace" (Jer. 6:13–14). Jeremiah was a small voice of truth is a sea of lies. "For both prophet and priest are profane; yea, in my house have I found their *wickedness* saith the LORD" (Jer. 23:11). For prophesying the truth, Jeremiah was persecuted by the priesthood, the prophets, the government, and the people. "Now it came to pass, when Jeremiah had ceased speaking all that the LORD had commanded him to speak unto all the people, that the priests and prophets and all the people took him, saying, Thou shalt surely die" (Jer. 26:8). "For then the king of Babylon's army besieged Jerusalem; and Jeremiah the prophet, was shut up in the court of the prison, which was in the king of Judah's house" (Jer. 32:2).

In both of these cases, God judged their iniquity. Both society's spiritual leaders, kings, and people moved from the values laid out in God's Word to the values established by the Amorites that were before them, leaving God completely out. God warned Israel hundreds of years before that if they defiled themselves with the "iniquity of the Amorites (Gen.15:16; Lev. 18:24) the land would vomit them out (Lev. 18:19–30). The abominations were idolatry, child sacrifice, homosexuality, spiritism, incest, and bestiality. The iniquity of these societies was full, and God judged them just as he judged all of civilization with the flood and the Amorites and Canaanites later. With the United States and the world matching the sins of iniquity committed by these societies sin for sin, iniquity for iniquity, do you think God will not judge the US and the world we now live in?

VII. The Deadly Spiral and Consequences of Iniquity

All of history shows nation after nation become more and more wicked, the longer they exist. Individually, man may repent; collectively, nations do not! There may be periods of national remorse and repentance as was with Israel and Nineveh (Jon. 3:5–10), but the spiral inevitably continues. When iniquity gets to the point where God ceases to tolerate it, He will destroy mankind as he did the pre-flood civilizations. When either a culture, people, or nation becomes so wicked their iniquity becomes full, God will destroy them as He did the Amorites (Gen. 15:6; Josh. 10:12–27). When the whole world's iniquity becomes full again as was in the days of Noah, Jesus will return smite the nations and set up his earthly kingdom. He will rule with a rod of iron as Lord of lords and King of kings for a thousand years. (Rev. 19:15–16, 21; 20:4). Where is the US and the world in their downward spiral?

VIII. Summary of the Mystery of Iniquity

1. Conceived by Satan
2. Believed by mankind
3. Imputed by the Law
4. Hindered by the Holy Spirit
5. Progressively gets worse with man's values and laws implemented.
6. Reaches its fullness when the Holy Spirit ceases to hinder.
7. Started by Satan, finished by God at the end of the 1,000-year reign. Reaches its end when Satan tempts the nations to rebel against Jesus at the end of the 1,000-year reign, and fire comes down from God and devours them; Satan is cast into the lake of fire (Rev. 20:7–10).

Chapter 10

The Mystery of the Kingdom of God

Mark 4:11; Luke 8:10; Matthew 6:33

I. **Context** (Matt. 13:10–11; Mark 4:10–11; Luke 8:9–10)

> ➤ The context of the usage of the phrases "kingdom of God" and kingdom of heaven."
> ➤ Mysteries of the kingdom of God only revealed to the believer.

II. **Defining the Kingdom of God:**

> ➤ Who is in the kingdom of God: It is universal including those willingly subject to the will of God? (Luke 13:28,29).
> ➤ What does God rule in His kingdom? Many are ruled but most are not in the kingdom of God.

1. God's rule over the nations.

   a) He is Governor among the nations (Ps 22: 28).
   b) God's kingdom is forever (Ps 45:6,145:13).
   c) The Most High rules in the kingdom of men and gives it to whoever he will (Dan. 4:17).
   d) God's kingdom will break in pieces the Gentile nations (Daniel 2:44).

      e) There is no power but of God (Rom. 13:1–2).

2. God rules all the earth (Ps. 66: 4–6).
3. God rules the raging sea (Ps. 89:9; Mark 4:39).
4. God rules over the spiritual domain (Job 1:6; Luke 4:31–37; Matt. 8:28–34).
5. God rules over sickness and death (2 Kings 20:1–11; John 11).

➤ When was the kingdom of God revealed to Israel? When Jesus was in the midst of them? The kingdom would not come with observation (Luke 17:20–21).

III. How does mankind discern the Kingdom of God? (1 Cor. 2:14)

➤ The kingdom of God is not understood by natural means or powers.
➤ It is spiritually discerned.

IV. How does a person enter the Kingdom of God?

➤ You must be born again of the spirit (John 3:3).
➤ By grace through faith. Works come after salvation (Eph. 2:5, 8).
➤ Only those who do the will of God will enter (Matt. 7:21).
➤ What is God's will? (John 6:40).
➤ Who will *not* enter the kingdom of God? (1 Cor. 6:9–11).

V. The Kingdom of God falls into two periods

1. The *present,* involving suffering and tribulation by the believer (Acts 14:22; Rom. 5:1–5; James 1:2–3).
2. The *future,* associated with the believer's reward and glory (Matt. 13:43; 25:34; Rev. 22:12).

The Mystery of the Kingdom of God
Mark 4:11; Luke 8:10; Matthew 6:33

I. Context: The gospel writers give reference to both the kingdom of God and the kingdom of heaven in the same settings. In some cases, they are interchangeable, and in other cases, they are not. In Matthew 13:10, Mark 4:10, and Luke 8:9, the writers are asking Jesus why He spoke to the people in parables? They ask, "Why speakest to them in parables," "The twelve asked of Him the parable," and "What might this parable be?" In Matthew 13:11, Jesus replied; "Because it is given unto you to know the mysteries of the kingdom of heaven, but to them it is not given." In Mark 4:11, Jesus replied; "Unto you it is given to know the mystery of the kingdom of God; but unto those who are outside, all these things are done in parables." In Luke 8:10, Jesus replied: "Unto you it is given to know the mysteries of the kingdom of God; but to others in parables, that seeing they might not see, and hearing they might not understand." In these cases, the Lord's intent is that those outside (the unbeliever) will neither understand the mysteries of the kingdom of God or the mysteries of the kingdom of heaven. An explanation of the two kingdoms is necessary for a clear understanding of the context of their usage.

II. Defining the Kingdom of God: All of creation are *under* the rule of the kingdom of God, but few are *in* the kingdom of God. An analogy would be a person who is in a country but not a citizen. The person must abide by the law of the country but does not receive the benefits of being a citizen. The subjects in the kingdom of God would be the obedient angels, the Church, and saints, both past and future. When Jesus was asked in Luke 13:23: "Lord, are there few that be saved?" Jesus told them of the strait gate that few enter in, and "There shall be weeping and gnashing of teeth, when ye shall see Abraham and Isaac, and Jacob and all the prophets, in the kingdom of God, and you yourselves thrust out. And they shall come from the east and from the

127

west, and from the north, and from the south, and shall sit down in the kingdom of God" (Luke 13:28–29). Only the believers and angels of God will be in the kingdom of God. All others, including Satan and his angels, will be ruled over by the kingdom of God but not in the kingdom of God.

The breakdown of all under the rule of the kingdom of God is the nations, the earth, the sea, the spiritual domain, and sickness and death. God rules everything in and outside His kingdom. God rules over the nations; "For the kingdom is the Lord's and he is the governor among the nations" (Ps. 24:28). God rules in the kingdom of men; "to the intent that the living may know that the most High ruleth in the kingdom of men, and giveth it to whomsoever he will, and setteth up over it the basest of men" (Dan. 4:17). God rules the earth: "All the earth shall worship thee, and shall sing unto thee; they shall sing to thy name. Selah" (Ps. 66:4). God rules the sea: "Thou rulest the raging of the sea: when the waves thereof arise, thou stillest them" (Ps. 89:9). God rules over the spiritual domain; "Now there was a day when the sons of God came to present themselves before the LORD, and Satan came also among them" (Job 1:6). Jesus demonstrated His power over the spiritual world when He cast out demons at Gadara (Matt. 8:28–34) and Capernaum (Luke 4:31–37). Finally, God demonstrated His rule over sickness and death when Hezekiah was healed (2 Kings 20:1–11) and when Jesus raised Lazarus from the dead (John 11).

The kingdom of God was revealed to Israel by the presence of the Lord Jesus Christ. In Luke 17:20–21, the Pharisees demanded of Jesus when the kingdom of God should come. Jesus replied: "The kingdom of God cometh not with observation. Neither shall they say, Lo here! Or, lo there! For, behold the kingdom of God is in the midst of you (within you)." In some King James translations, the word used by Jesus to communicate location is *midst*; in others it is *within.* Both define the location. The Greek word is *entos* (ἐντός), and denotes within or among.[20] At that time the King was in the midst or among the Pharisees who asked the question, and the kingdom of God was not within those asking the question. For the kingdom of God to be within a person that person must be a believer. The word Jesus used identifies while at the same time condemns the Pharisees.

III. How Does Mankind Discern the Kingdom of God? (1 Cor. 2:14). As Jesus answered the question posed by the Pharisees, He knew they could not understand His answer, for they were spiritually blind. In the letter to the Corinthians, Paul said: "But the natural man receiveth not the things of the Spirit of God; for they are foolishness unto him, neither can he know them, because they ae spiritually discerned." These Pharisees were ruled by the kingdom of God, but they could not see the kingdom of God and were not in the kingdom of God.

IV. How Does a Person Enter the Kingdom of God? (John 3). The answers Jesus gave were very puzzling to the Pharisees. That is probably why Nicodemus, a ruler of the Jews and a Pharisee, came to Jesus at night. Nicodemus realized Jesus could not be doing the miracles witnessed by so many without the power of God. When Jesus told Nicodemus that he must be born again in order to see the kingdom of God, Nicodemus said; "How can these things be" (John 3:9)? Jesus further explained what was meant by being born again and how "God so loved the world, that he gave his only begotten Son that whosoever believeth in him should not perish but have everlasting life" (John 3:16). In John 19:39, the scripture records Nicodemus assisting Joseph of Arimathea in the burial preparation after the crucifixion of Jesus. Nicodemus had moved from being ruled by the kingdom of God to being in the kingdom of God as a child and heir of God (Rom. 8:17).

---

[20] W.E. Vine, *Expository Dictionary of New Testament Words.*

Nicodemus had been saved by grace through faith in Jesus and not by the self-righteous works of the law that the Pharisees thought was necessary to be acceptable to God (Eph. 2:5,8). Nicodemus possibly heard the words of Jesus when he said in Matthew 7:21: "Not everyone that saith unto me, Lord, Lord, shall enter into the kingdom of heaven; but he that doeth the will of my Father in heaven." What is the will of the Father? It is believing and accepting Jesus Christ as Lord and Savior. "And this is the will of him that sent me, that everyone which seeth the Son, and believeth on him, may have everlasting life: and I will raise him up at the last day" (John 6:40).

A distinction between the kingdom of God and the kingdom of heaven is worthy of note when considering Matthew 7:21. The original Greek is the kingdom of the heavens (ovpαvῶV),[21] meaning the eternal dwelling place of God and can be rendered either the kingdom of God or the kingdom of heaven. God is in both, but for a person to enter the dwelling place of God, they must be saved. Here lies one of the confusing usages of the two phrases.

Most confusion surfaces when in the same context, Matthew uses the term kingdom of heaven, and the other gospel writers use the term kingdom of God. The key is to look at the kingdom of God as God's total domain of rule, that is, all creation, heaven, earth, angels, and mankind. Even the lake of fire (hell) is within God's domain for He created it for Satan and his followers. The kingdom of heaven is within the domain of the kingdom of God. There is no ambiguity, however, when Matthew recorded what Jesus said: "But seek ye first the kingdom of God, and his righteousness; and all these things will be added unto you" (Matt. 6:33). Man needs to seek first the kingdom of God for it is spiritual (Rom. 14:17). The kingdom of heaven is Messianic and fulfills the promise by God to David when Jesus returns and sets up His

---

millennial reign. If a person is not in the kingdom of God, they will not participate in the millennial reign unless they are born during the millennial reign. That is made plain by the tares among the wheat and the good and bad fish illustrated in Matthew 13. The tares were destroyed, and the bad fish were cast out. Mankind is born into the kingdom of God only through the spiritual birth. If a person seeks only the kingdom of heaven, the extension of the Davidic kingdom, as the Pharisees, Sadducees and Herodians did and not the kingdom of God, they will be burned as tares and cast aside as bad fish.

For the believer who is studying the mysteries, it is just as important to know who will enter the kingdom of God as it is to know those who will not enter God's kingdom. We live in a perverted society that calls good evil and evil good. In the society of the twenty-first century, those who are novices in the scripture can be led to believe whoever puts a label of *"church"* on their doctrine are saved. That is absolutely untrue. To be an effective witness, the believer must be well equipped with the Word of God. Some congregations today, calling themselves Christian, embrace homosexuality and in fact have homosexual clergy. Some congregations wink at adultery and fornication, while others who are more sophisticated are steeped in idolatry. Specifically, the idolatry of power as exhibited by many of the nation's leaders who will do anything to gain and sustain power. That thirst for power includes support of the murder of the unborn in order to gain votes and a global agenda that moves the world closer and closer to a ripe society, awaiting God's wrath.

Paul makes very clear those who will not enter the kingdom of God with his letter to the Corinthians. This was a society that the United States and the world now mirror. Paul said in 1 Corinthians 6:9–11:

> "Know ye not that the unrighteous shall not inherit the kingdom of God? Be not deceived: neither fornicators,

nor idolaters, nor adulterers, nor effeminate, nor abusers of themselves with mankind, Nor thieves, nor covetous, nor drunkards, nor revilers, nor extortioners, shall inherit the kingdom of God. And such were some of you: but ye are washed, but ye are sanctified, but ye are justified in the name of the Lord Jesus, and by the Spirit of our God."

Who in this list has the very law of the land supported and protected? Liars, they are the congress and the president who are immune from accountability for lying if not under oath (Rev. 22:15). Effeminate, they are homosexuals protected under the law in marriage and any form of perceived discrimination. Abusers of themselves with mankind, they are the transgenders who, with dogma and surgery, attempt to redefine gender. Revilers, they are the politicians and news media who distort, lie, and criticize that which is good under the guise of freedom of speech and freedom of the press.

Paul was plainly telling the Corinthians that those who were habitual in these sins would not inherit the kingdom of God. They would go to hell. However, many had turned from their sin and were saved. That was true then, and it is true now. However, the believer must not replace the Word of God with the politically correct things of today. Christians must be bold in their witness and not cower to the pressure of society.

VI. The Kingdom of God Falls Into Two Time Periods: The first period is while the believer is living on earth prior to their death or the rapture. Many babes in Christ are confused when various situations engulf them and life catches them off guard. God never promised a life without trials and tribulation. James encouraged the believer who was faced with such: "My brethren count it all joy when ye fall into various trials, Knowing this, that the testing of your faith worketh patience. But let patience have her perfect work, that ye may be perfect and entire, lacking nothing "(James 1:2–3). Paul made the connection between tribulation, patience, and hope for the believer in his letter to the Romans:

> "Therefore being justified by faith, we have peace with God through our Lord Jesus Christ: by whom also we have access by faith into this grace wherein we stand and rejoice in hope of the glory of God. And not only so, but we glory in tribulations also: knowing that tribulation worketh patience; And patience, experience; and experience hope: And hope maketh not ashamed; because the love of God is shed abroad in our hearts by the Holy Ghost which is given unto us." (Rom. 5:1–5)

Paul was well exposed and experienced with trials and tribulation as demonstrated by his letter to the Romans. When he was stoned at Lystra, he continued his work, "Confirming the souls of the disciples and exhorting them to continue in the faith, and that we must through tribulation enter into the kingdom of God" (Acts 14:22). The believer in the present age should not be overcome with the things of the world and lose their witness to the lost. Paul said in Romans 14:16–17: "Let not then your good be evil spoken of: For the kingdom of God is not meat and drink; but righteousness, and peace, and joy in the Holy Ghost."

The second period for the believer in the kingdom of God is that time of receiving glory, inheritance and reward. Jesus said in Matthew 13:43, "Then shall the righteous shine forth as the sun in the kingdom of their father." Jesus said in Matthew 25:34, "Then shall the King say unto them on his right hand, Come, ye blessed of my Father, inherit the kingdom prepared for you from the foundation of the world:" Jesus spoke of the reward of the believer while preaching the sermon on the mount (Matt. 5:12). Paul spoke of the reward of the believer who builds on the foundation of Jesus Christ in his letter to the Corinthians (1 Cor. 3:8–14) and in the last book of the Bible, John records the words of Jesus when He said: "And behold, I come quickly; and my reward is with me, to give every man according as his work shall be" (Rev. 22:12). There will be for the believer trials and tribulations on earth, but there will be in the kingdom of God an inheritance and a reward for the believer as the glory of God and the glory of the bride of Christ shows forth in the New Jerusalem (Rev. 21).

Chapter 11

The Mysteries of the Kingdom of Heaven

Matthew 3:2; Mark 1:3–8

I. Context

> ➤ The kingdom of God is spiritual (John 3:3).
> ➤ The kingdom of heaven is according to the flesh and is earthly (2 Sam. 7:1–17).

II. What Is the Kingdom of Heaven?

> ➤ The kingdom of heaven shows the rule of Messiah over the earth (Dan. 2:31–44).

1. It will stand forever (v. 44).
2. This rule is indicated in the Lord's prayer. "Thy kingdom come thy will be done in earth, as it is in heaven" (Matt. 6:10).
3. It is in opposition to earthly rule and defined in Daniel as the kingdom which "the God of Heaven" will set up after the destruction by "the stone cut out without hands." This is the destruction of the Gentile world empires (Dan. 2:34–36, 44).

4. It is the fulfillment of God's covenant with David and his decedents.

➤ The kingdom of heaven will be established at the second coming of Christ (Luke 1:32–33, Rev. 20:4–6).
➤ The Jews are blind to the reality of a suffering servant who could be their king (Isa. 53).
➤ The kingdom of heaven is used dispensationally and is connected to Israel (Matt. 3:2).

III. Reconciling the Kingdom of Heaven and the Kingdom of God in the Same Parables

➤ Do the parables apply to the church age? (Matt. 13:19; Mark 4:15; Rev. 20:3).
➤ When are the use of the phrases kingdom of God and kingdom of heaven *not* interchangeable?

1. Parable of the Wheat and Tares (Matt. 13:24–30)Only in the kingdom of heaven.
2. Parable of the Dragnet (Matt. 13:47–50)Only in the kingdom of heaven.
3. What to seek first (Matt. 6:33, John 3:3)Only the kingdom of God.

IV. What the Mystery of the Kingdom of Heaven Reveals

The Mysteries of the Kingdom of Heaven
Matthew 3:2; Mark 1:3–8

I. Context: There are distinctive differences in the kingdom of God and the kingdom of heaven. Therefore, there are differences in their mysteries. As already pointed out in the mystery of the kingdom of

God, the kingdom of God includes all moral intelligent beings that are willing to be subject to the will of God. This would include, the four living creatures (Rev. 4:6), angels, Old Testament saints, church-age saints, and those who will receive Christ as Lord and Savior after the Church is raptured and during the tribulation and millennial reign. Entry into the kingdom of God is only through the spiritual birth (John 3:3). The kingdom of God is spiritual.

The kingdom of heaven in its fullness is the fulfillment of God's promise to David through the prophet Nathan. King David spoke to the prophet Nathan of his desire to build a house for the Lord. God, through a vision, spoke to Nathan and told him to tell David He would establish the kingdom of David forever, and He would establish David's throne forever (2 Sam. 7:1–17). At the end of the tribulation, God will set the stage for the fulfillment of His promise to David by destroying all the nations that come against Israel (Zech. 12:8–9). The fulfillment of God's promise to David will occur during the millennial reign of the Messiah, Jesus Christ (Rev. 20:6). The covenant God made with David will be fulfilled through Jesus Christ, the Son of David, and will result in the establishment of the kingdom of heaven. The kingdom of heaven is according to the flesh and is the earthly pinnacle of the Davidic kingdom.

II. What Is the Kingdom of Heaven? First, it is called the kingdom of heaven because it shows the rule of the heavens over the earth. This is indicated by Jesus in His prayer; "Thy kingdom come. Thy will be done in earth, as it is in heaven" (Matt. 6:10). It is in opposition to the rule by man on earth and explained by Daniel (Dan. 2:31–43). When Nebuchadnezzar had a dream of a great, terrible image, and the dream had gone from him, he asked the magicians and astrologers and sorcerers to, not only interpret the dream, but tell him what the dream was. They could not, but God revealed the dream in a vision to Daniel, and he interpreted it to Nebuchadnezzar. The dream was of a great, terrible image made of different metals with feet of iron and clay. A stone cut out without hands smote the image upon his feet that were of iron and clay and boke them to pieces. All the material became like chaff and was blown away by the wind. Daniel gave Nebuchadnezzar the interpretation, revealing to him the parts of the image was the different world Gentile empires that God would destroy and replace with a kingdom that would stand forever. "And in the day of these kings shall the God of heaven set up a kingdom, which shall never be destroyed: and the kingdom shall not be left to other people, but it shall break in pieces and consume all these kingdoms, and it shall stand for ever" (Dan. 2:44).

The stone cut out without hands was not revealed to Daniel. However, Paul and Peter revealed the stone to be the chief cornerstone and the foundation of the Church (Eph. 2:20; 1 Pet. 2:6). It is Jesus Christ. Paul said it was a stumbling stone to the Jews (Rom. 9:32). At Christ's second coming, He is the headstone of the corner (Zech. 4:7), and to the unbeliever, Jesus is the stone of judgment (Matt. 21:44). Jesus Christ is identified in Revelation 19:16 as the KING OF KINGS AND LORD OF LORDS. He is the King of the kingdom of heaven.

Second, this earthly rule will be established at the second coming of Christ as He sets up His thousand-year reign (Rev. 20:4–6). This was confirmed to Mary by the angel Gabriel prior to the birth of Jesus. "He shall be great, and shall be called the Son of the Highest: and the Lord God shall give unto him the throne of his father David: And he shall reign over the house of Jacob for ever; and of his kingdom there shall be no end" (Luke 1:32–33).

Third, the kingdom of heaven is the Messiah's rule over the earth. The rule of Messiah over the earth and the reestablishment of the Davidic kingdom is what the Jews were looking for when Jesus walked among them. They could not understand their Messiah as being a suffering servant as the prophet Isaiah had told them in Isaiah 53. They were blind and only looked for a conquering king who would throw off the yoke of

Roman dominance. They rejected the Savior and are still looking for the Messiah. The rule will begin at the end of the tribulation period and the first resurrection and will last for 1,000 years. At the end of the thousand-year reign, the great white throne judgment will take place at the second resurrection (Rev. 20:11–15), and the old heaven and earth will be burned up and replaced with a new heaven and earth (Rev. 21:1–2). The kingdom will be delivered up and merged with the kingdom of God so that God (Father, Son, Holy Spirit) will be all in all (1 Cor. 15:24–28).

Fourth, the kingdom of heaven is used only dispensationally and in connection to Israel. The kingdom was announced to be at hand by John the Baptist (Matt. 3:2), but the King was rejected. Before the rejection and crucifixion, Christ established His Church. We are now in the Church age, which will end when Christ raptures His Church. Following the rapture of the Church and during the tribulation period, the 144,000 Jews will be sealed to again preach the Gospel of the kingdom of heaven. At the end of the tribulation, Christ will return with His bride, the Church, crush all earthly powers, and set up his earthly kingdom. At that time, the kingdom of heaven will be in place, with Christ ruling with a rod of Iron. The Old Testament saints, the Church, and those saved during the tribulation period will enter the kingdom of heaven (Christ's kingdom on earth) and rule with Christ as judges and priest for a thousand years. The explanation and scripture of the preceding dispensation order is given in:

1. The Mystery of Christ and the Church;
2. The Mystery of the Gospel;
3. The Mystery of Israel's Blindness; and
4. The Mystery of the Resurrection.

III. Reconciling the Kingdom of Heaven and the Kingdom of God in the Same Parables: If the kingdom of heaven is dispensational and it will come into power only when Christ returns with his bride, the Church, do the statements and parables Jesus spoke to the disciples and Jewish religious leaders apply to the Church age? With both kingdoms having almost all things in common and used in some parables interchangeably, how does the believer know when they must be consistent and specific? The chart below references many of the parables and statements Jesus made. Matthew, most of the time, uses the term kingdom of heaven while Mark and Luke use the term kingdom of God.

Use of the Phrases Kingdom of Heaven and Kingdom of God				
Parable/Topic	Matthew	Mark	Luke	John
Sower	13:1–23, Heaven	4:1–20, God	8:4–15, God	Omitted
Tares	13:24–30, heaven	Omitted	Omitted	Omitted
Mustard Seed	13:31–32 Heaven	4:30–32, God	13:18–19, God	Omitted
Leaven	13:33, Heaven	Omitted	13:20–21, God	Omitted
Hidden Treasure	13:44, Heaven	Omitted	Omitted	Omitted
Pearl	13:45–46, Heaven	Omitted	Omitted	Omitted
Dragnet	13:47–50, Heaven	Omitted	Omitted	Omitted
Unnoticed growth	Omitted	4:26–29, God	Omitted	Omitted
Seek first	6:33, God	Omitted	Omitted	Omitted
See or enter	Omitted	Omitted	Omitted	3:3–5, God

Although the kingdom of heaven will be established at Christ's second coming, there are two reasons the reference to the kingdom of heaven applies to the Church age:

1. In the Parable of the Sower, the one who takes away the Word, the seed, is the wicked one (Matt. 13:19), Satan (Mark 4:15), and the Devil (Luke 8:12). Satan will not be able to take away the Word during the millennial reign, for he is bound the full thousand years. Therefore, Jesus is speaking of the Church age when Satan is allowed to influence the world with his wickedness. In fact, John said in 1 John 5:19, "And we know that we are of God, and the whole world lieth in wickedness."

2. The omission in the kingdom of God of the Parables of the Tares and the Dragnet are significant because they are only referenced as being the kingdom of heaven. The tares are separated from the wheat and burned, and the bad fish are separated from the good fish and cast out. There will be separation of the real and false professions in the kingdom of heaven. There are no tares or bad fish in the kingdom of God; they are only in the kingdom of heaven.

Many of the parables use the two kingdoms interchangeably. This occurs because the kingdom of heaven is the earthly spere of the universal kingdom of God. However, when it comes to seeking what really matters, Matthew said; "Seek ye first the kingdom of God" (Matt. 6:33), not the kingdom of heaven. For the kingdom of heaven is earthly where the kingdom of God is spiritual, and the only way to enter the kingdom of God is through the new spiritual birth (John 3:3).

IV. Other Characteristics of the Kingdom of Heaven

1. If a person is in the kingdom of God, they will be in the kingdom of heaven during the millennial reign.

2. A person can be in the kingdom of heaven but not in the kingdom of God. This is revealed not only by the parables of the tares and wheat and the good and bad fish, but those who follow Satan at the end of the thousand-year reign. They had lived during the reign of Christ but followed Satan when he was released from the abyss to tempt the nations. Again, this shows the mystery of faith.

3. There were those who rejected Jesus when the kingdom of heaven was at hand. There will be those who will reject the Gospel of the kingdom during the tribulation, and there will be those who will reject the King of kings and embrace Satan, showing just how depraved and evil mankind can be.

4. The climax of the kingdom of heaven is when Christ rules supreme, putting all enemies under His feet, including death, and then delivering up the kingdom to God the Father. When this is complete, the kingdom of heaven and the kingdom of God will be one with God being all in all; Father, Son, and Holy Spirit (1 Cor. 15:24–28)

5. Neither the mysteries of the kingdom of heaven nor the mystery of the kingdom of God are discerned by natural man. Only the spirit-filled believer is capable of understanding the mysteries.

Chapter 12

The Mystery of God's Will

Ephesians 1:3–14

I. Context: The mystery of God's will in light of His sovereignty and man's free will (Eph. 1:4–5)

- ➢ God's election and predestination of the believer.
- ➢ God's choices before man was created.
- ➢ Does man have the freedom to choose?

II. Words and examples that help define God's Sovereignty

- ➢ God's sovereignty and King Nebuchadnezzar (Dan. 4).
- ➢ God's sovereignty and Cyrus the Great (Isa. 44–46).
- ➢ Biblical meaning of words that define sovereignty:

    1. Adoption
    2. Election
    3. Foreknowledge
    4. Predestinate
    5. Purpose
    6. Redemption

➢ Does the doctrine of Calvinism explain God's sovereignty and God's will?

1. Five Points of Calvinism.
2. Peter's warning! Study God's Word in its total context (2 Pet. 1:20).

III. God's will versus man's free will: Word meanings that matter!

➢ Will (Matt. 18:11, 14; Eph. 1:11)
➢ Willing (2 Pet. 3:9)
➢ All (John 3:16; Acts 17:30)
➢ World
➢ Everyone

IV. How does God's sovereignty and will align with the free will of man?

➢ Angels were created with the freedom to choose (Isa. 14:13–14; Ezek. 28:12–17).
➢ Mankind was created with the freedom to choose:

1. Adam and Eve (Gen. 3).
2. Cain (Gen. 4).
3. The pre-flood generation (Gen. 6).

➢ God strove with man, but man resisted God's grace.

V. How does God's Spirit strive with mankind?

➢ Through God's visible creation (Rom. 1).
➢ Through God's law (Gal. 3).
➢ Through the blood of Christ sacrificed for our sins (Luke 19:10).

> Through the Holy Spirit (John 16).
> Through the Gospels, with the last being the everlasting Gospel (Rev. 14).

VI. Summary

> Understanding the mystery of God's will through the "dispensation of times" (Eph. 1:10; 1 Cor. 15:24).
> The order of the ages ordained by God.
> The fundamental measurement of time is change.
> God does not change (Heb. 13:8).
> God created time and is not bound by His creation.
> God sees past, present, and future.
> God can elect, predestinate, and purpose because of His foreknowledge.

The Mystery of God's Will
Ephesians 1:3–14

I. *Context:* In Paul's letter to the Ephesians, a very complex doctrine is presented. It is the mystery of God's will. In Ephesians 1:9, Paul states: "Having made known unto us the mystery of his will, according to his good pleasure which he hath purposed in himself." The statement is surrounded by verses that include words like chosen or election (v. 4), predestinated and adoption (v. 5), redemption (v. 7), and purpose (v. 11). How should Christians approach the study of their election, predestination, redemption, and adoption by God in the context of the mystery of God's will as well as Ephesians 1:4? "According as he hath chosen us in him before the foundation of the world, that we should be holy without blame before him, in love." How is it that God chose the believer before He created him? Does this mean man had no choice or free will? How should the believer view the sovereignty of God and the freewill of man in light of what the Bible says?

II. Words That Help Define God's Sovereignty: The modern-day definition of sovereignty is supreme power or authority. God has the power to create something from nothing. The Hebrew word is *bara*, used in Genesis 1:1: "In the beginning God created the heaven and earth." When it comes to power, Paul puts the power of God in the proper context with that of man's power. Romans 13:1 states: "Let every soul be subject unto higher powers. For there is no power but of God the powers that be are ordained of God." All power that either a person, a law, an organization, or a nation may have, is only allowed and made manifest by the power of God. Two examples of God's sovereignty imposed on individuals are that of King Nebuchadnezzar of Babylon and Cyrus the Great of Persia. Both men, in their time, were the most powerful individuals on the face of the earth.

In Daniel 4, Nebuchadnezzar dreamed a dream of a great tree being cut down by a holy one from heaven. The stump was not destroyed but was reserved to regenerate. Daniel interpreted the dream to the king and said the tree exemplified the king who was a great man upon the earth. Further, Daniel told the king he would be driven from his rule to eat grass with the beasts of the field for a period of seven times. The king would be given the heart of a beast, with his hair growing like eagles' feathers and his nails like birds' claws (v. 33) until he acknowledged the God of creation. The reason God did this to Nebuchadnezzar is recorded in verses 17, 25, and 32: "to the intent that the living may know that the Most High ruleth in the kingdom of men, and giveth it to whomsoever he will, and setteth up over it the basest of men." The vision was fulfilled and the king was struck down when he said, "Is not this great Babylon that I have built for the house of the kingdom by the might of my power, and for the honor of my majesty?" (v. 30). When the times ended, Nebuchadnezzar acknowledged who rules and reigns and praised God (v. 34) and God restored him. The king learned "The fear of the LORD is to hate evil, pride, and arrogance, and the evil way, and the perverse mouth do I hate" (Prov. 8:13).

In Isaiah 44:28–45:1, before the southern kingdom went into captivity by the Babylonians, Isaiah prophesied of Cyrus the Great. The prophecy was that Cyrus would restore Jerusalem and rebuild the temple. This happened during the time of Ezra and Nehemiah.

> "Who saith of Cyrus, He is my shepherd, and shall perform all my pleasure; even saying to Jerusalem, Thou shalt be built; and to the temple, Thy foundation shall be laid. Thus saith the LORD to his anointed, to Cyrus, whose right hand I have held, to subdue nations before him; and I will loose the loins of kings, to open before him the two-leaved gates; and the gates shall not be shut."

Then Isaiah says in 46:11, speaking of Cyrus: "Calling a ravenous bird from the east, the man that executeth my counsel from a far country; yea I have spoken it I will also bring it to pass; I have purposed it, I will also do it." Isaiah prophesied around 740 BC. Cyrus was born in 600 BC. Therefore, through God's sovereignty, He purposed the name of Cyrus and what he would do 140 years before he was born.

God, through His foreknowledge, and sovereignty purposed what both Nebuchadnezzar and Cyrus would do. To gain some understanding of God's sovereignty (power) is to understand the words used to describe His power over His creation, over time and space and His power to save us from our sin. Following are some of those words:

3. **Adoption:** the Greek word for adoption is *huiothesia* (υἱοθεσία). It means to place, signifies the place and condition of a son given to one to whom it does not naturally belong[22] (Eph. 1:5).

---

[22]   W.E. Vine, *Expository Dictionary of New Testament Words.*

4. **Election:** the Greek word for election is *ekloge* (ἐκλογή) denotes a picking out, selection, that which is chosen[23] (Eph. 1:4). In 1 Peter 1:2, Peter is speaking to the elect according to the *foreknowledge of God.* "Elect according to the foreknowledge of God, the Father, through sanctification of the Spirit, unto obedience and sprinkling of the blood of Jesus Christ: Grace unto you and peace, be multiplied."

5. **Foreknowledge:** the Greek word for foreknowledge is *proginosko* (προγινώσκ?) To know before, used of divine knowledge. Also, the Greek word *prognosis* (πρόγνωσις) an aspect of omniscience implied in God's warnings, promises and predictions.[24] Acts 15:18 states: "Known unto God are all his works from the beginning of the world." In Romans 8:29, *foreknowledge is the prerequisite to predestinate:* "For whom he did foreknow he also did predestinate to be conformed to the image of his Son, that he might be the firstborn among many brethren."

6. **Predestinate:** the Greek word *proorizo* (προορίζω) implies God's foreknowledge and means to determine.[25] Believers are predestinated according to the purpose of God, as in Ephesians 1:11, "In whom also we have obtained an inheritance, being predestinated *according to the purpose of him* who worketh all things after the counsel of his own will." Predestination applies only to the believer. Nowhere in scripture is there any indication that God predestinates a person to hell (lake of fire).

7. **Purpose:** the Greek word is *prothesis* (πρόθεσις), meaning a setting forth. Also, the Greek word is *protithemi* (προτίθημι)

---

23 Ibid.

24 Ibid.

25 Ibid.

meaning foreordained.[26] Concerning the judgment of Assyria: "For the LORD of hosts hath purposed, and who shall annul it? And his hand is stretched out, and who shall turn it back?" Romans 8:28 says: "And we know that all things work together for good to them that love God, to them who are the called according to his purpose." In Romans 9:11–13, concerning Esau and Jacob, the Word says: "(For the children being not yet born, neither having done any good or evil, that the purpose of God according to election might stand, not of words, but of him that calleth), It was said unto her, The elder shall serve the younger. As it is written, Jacob have I loved and Esau have I hated." In 2 Timothy 1:9, Paul is reminding Timothy of what God has done in their lives: "Who hath saved us, and called us with an holy calling, not according to our works, but according to his purpose and grace which was given us in Christ Jesus before the world began," Throughout the Bible God's purpose is demonstrated. All these statements by men of the Bible conclude God's purpose will be done. However, does that mean man has no choice in the matter?

8. **Redemption:** the Greek word is *apolutrosis* (ἀπολντρωσις), meaning a releasing for payment of a ransom[27] or deliverance from physical torture (Eph. 1:7).

A study of these words along with the examples of God's work in the lives of Esau and Jacob, King Nebuchadnezzar, and Cyrus the Great would lead one to the conclusion that John Calvin's five points of Calvinism is unquestionable Bible doctrine. Calvin proposed the following:[28]

---

[26] Ibid.

[27] Ibid.

[28] Bob Kirkland D.D., *Calvinism None Dare Call It Heresy.*

Total Depravity, meaning man is completely and wholly depraved and has no ability whatsoever to respond (repent or believe) to God until he is first regenerated by God.

Unconditional Election, meaning God determined before the foundation of the world whom He would save and whom He would send to hell. Man would have no choice or free will to either accept or reject Christ as Savior.

Limited Atonement, meaning Christ's atonement on the Cross was not for everyone but rather just for the elect.

Irresistible Grace, meaning faith is something "God irresistibly bestowed upon the elect without their having believed anything and by such reasoning man cannot even hear the gospel much less respond to the pleadings of Christ."

Perseverance of the Saints, meaning the emphasis is upon the believer's faithfulness in persevering, not God's power. Uncertainty of a person's salvation is part of the fabric of the doctrine.

The case for concluding that man has no choice as to his destiny could be drawn if only these words and verses were considered. Yet again, Peter's warning is timely: "Knowing this first, that no prophecy of the scripture is of any private interpretation." (2 Pet. 1:20). Yes, first we must look at the total context of God's Word, not picking and choosing, but looking for God's complete message. Does God's sovereignty and will completely override the free will of man?

III. God's Will versus Man's Free Will: That brings the study of God's will and man's free will to the forefront, and again word definitions matter.

1. **Will:** in the Greek is *thelema* (θελημα) and speaks of God's will, which means the gracious design rather than the determined resolve.[29] Synonyms are desire, determination, choice, and inclination.[30] In Ephesians 1:9, Paul wrote: "Having made known unto us the mystery of his *will.* According to his good pleasure which he hath purposed in himself." Then in Ephesians 1:11, Paul wrote: "In whom also we have obtained an inheritance, being predestinated according to the purpose of him who worketh all things after the counsel of his own *will.*" The key is to understand the meaning of the words God's will. Example: In Matthew 18:11, 14, "For the Son of Man is come to save that which was lost ... Even so it is not the *will* of your Father which is in heaven, that one of these little ones should perish."

2. **Willing:** in the Greek is *prothumos* (πρόθυμος) or *hekousios* (έκονσιος), which mean ready or of free will.[31] Second Peter 3:9 says: "The Lord is not slack concerning his promise, as some men count slackness; but is longsuffering to us-ward, not *willing* that any should perish, but that *all* should come to repentance."

3. **All:** in the Greek is *pantos* (παντωs), meaning wholly, entirely, every kind or variety.[32] In Acts 17:30, Paul at Athens on Mar's Hill states: "And the times of this ignorance God winked at; but now commandeth *all* men everywhere to repent."

---

[29] W.E. Vine, *Expository Dictionary of New Testament Words.*

[30] James Strong; LL.D., S.T.D., *Exhaustive Concordance Of The Bible.*

[31] Ibid.

[32] Ibid.

In John 3:16, the original Greek says: "For so loved God the *world* that his Son the only begotten he gave, that *everyone* who believes on him may not perish but have life eternal."

4. **World:** in the Greek is *kosmos* (κόσμος), meaning the human race, mankind.[33]

5. **Everyone:** in the Greek is *pas* (πας), meaning any and every, of every kind. [34]

IV. How Does God's Sovereignty and Will Align with Man's Free Will?

Does God's sovereignty preclude His will and man's free will? The scripture provides a sequence of events that illustrate how God has given the angelic host and mankind the free will to choose. When God created the heavenly host, He gave them the ability to choose. The Bible speaks of Michael the archangel (Jude 9), Gabriel (meaning man of God; Dan. 9:16), cherubim (Gen. 3:24), Seraphim (Isa. 6:2), and Satan, the anointed cherub. Out of these angels, Satan and the angels that followed him chose to rebel against God. "For thou hast said in thine heart, I will ascend into heaven, I will exalt my throne above the stars of God: I will sit also upon the mount of the congregation, in the sides of the north: I will ascend above the heights of the clouds; I will be like the most High" (Isa. 14:13–14). "Thou wast perfect in thy ways from the day that thou wast created, till iniquity was found in thee" (Ezek. 28:12–17). Satan (Lucifer) along with the angels that followed him clearly chose a path of destruction.

Just as God gave the angelic host a free will, He gave man the ability to choose. Man was created in the image of God. Therefore, as God chose to love man, man has a choice to trust and obey God or doubt

---

[33]   Ibid.

[34]   Ibid.

and rebel against God. Adam and Eve chose to disobey God and sin. Cain chose to rebel against God and kill Abel in jealousy and hatred and then chose to go out from the presence of the Lord (Gen. 3–4). All of mankind from Adam to Noah chose to rebel against God, "And the LORD said, My Spirit shall not always strive with man, for that he also is flesh: yet his days shall be an hundred and twenty years" (Gen. 6:3).

> "And God saw that the wickedness of man was great in the earth, and that every imagination of the thoughts of his heart was only evil continually. And it repented the Lord that he had made man on the earth, and it grieved him at his heart. And the LORD said, I will destroy man whom I have created from the face of the earth; both man, and beast, and the creeping thing, and the fowls of the air; for it repenteth me that I have made them." (Gen. 6:5–7)

This is not irresistible grace. God gave man *the power of choice* while His Spirit strives with man by His grace to draw mankind in faith, belief, and obedience to Himself.

V. How Does God's Spirit Strive with Mankind? First, if God has pre-determined who would go to heaven and who would go to hell, why would He strive with mankind? Second, in what ways does God strive and seek to draw mankind to Himself?

1. Through God's visible creation God seeks mankind (Rom. 1:20): "For the invisible things of him from the creation of the world are clearly seen, being understood by the things that are made, even his eternal power and Godhead; so that they are without excuse." This means man has a choice. That choice, throughout time has degraded into the rationalization of existence due to everything but the God of creation. Mythical gods have been

imagined, a big bang has been hypothesized, evolution has been proposed, and global apocalypse with salvage by only man's intervention is now proposed with a "green new deal." Foolishness before the flood, foolishness after the flood, foolishness now, and foolishness until the Lord Jesus returns. Man is without excuse!

2. Through the Law, God seeks mankind (Gal. 3:24–25): "Wherefore the law was our schoolmaster to bring us unto Christ, that we might be justified by faith. But after that faith is come, we are no longer under a schoolmaster." A schoolmaster in ancient Greece was the person who brought the children into the classroom for learning. He was the source for getting the child in the place to learn, not the subject to learn. That is what the Law does. It shows man the righteous will of God, and the judgments that God will impose if His will is not obeyed. It shows man it is impossible to meet God's standards and shows man he needs a savior to keep him from God's judgments. The Law condemns man and points and draws him to Jesus Christ for salvation.

3. Through the birth, life, death, burial, resurrection, and ascension of Jesus Christ, man is sought by God. Jesus said: "For the son of man is come to seek and to save that which was lost" (Luke 19:10). He is walking with and seeking the lost, all of the lost.

4. Through His Holy Spirit God seeks mankind (John 16:8–11). Although the Holy Spirit strives with the lost by convicting them, many will choose not to receive the Gospel of grace. Many will resist the Holy Spirit, as in Acts 7:51: "Ye Stiff-necked and uncircumcised in heart and ears, ye do always resist the Holy Spirit as your fathers did so, so do ye." This is not irresistible grace.

5. Through the Gospel of the kingdom, the Gospel of grace and the everlasting Gospel, God has and will seek mankind. During the tribulation, when the everlasting Gospel is preached by an angel (Rev. 14:6–7), many will reject Christ, even up to and including when the last judgment is poured out. When the seventh vial judgment is poured out, it is proclaimed "It Is Done" (Rev. 16:17). God will seek man up to the end.

In all of these efforts, God is either trying to get people to repent and turn to him of their own free will, or God enjoys punishing those He has doomed to hell. When the will and sovereignty of God is examined and compared to the free will of man, there seems to be a dilemma. Can there be a reconciliation? Here in lies the mystery of God's will.

VI. Summary: Going back to Ephesians 1:3–14, God chose us before the foundation of the earth (v. 4). God predestinated us into the adoption of sons by Jesus Christ to Himself, according to the good pleasure of his will (v. 5). We have been accepted by God because of what Jesus did on the cross (v. 6). We have redemption through Christ's blood, the forgiveness of sins, according to the riches of his grace (v. 7). As a believer and part of the family of God, we are uniquely capable of understanding the mystery of His will. In what way can we understand the mystery of His will? "That in the dispensation of the fullness of times he might gather together in one all things in Christ, both which are in heaven, and which are on earth even in him" (v. 10). When will that happen? "Then cometh the end, when he shall have delivered up the kingdom to God, even the Father; when he shall have put down all rule and all authority and power" (1 Cor. 15:24). It will happen at the end of His thousand-year reign.

Therefore, one of the keys to understanding the mystery is the context of "The fullness of times." They are the ordered ages ordained by God which condition human life on earth. They are: innocence (Gen.

1:28), conscience (Gen. 3:7), human government (Gen. 8:15), promise (Gen. 12:1), Law (Exod. 19:1), Church (Acts 2:1), and the kingdom age (thousand-year reign; Rev. 20:4). All of these ages are bounded by a time period. We as human beings measure, abide by and age as time passes. From the beginning of creation, time has been measured by change. The sun comes up, the moon appears, the seasons change. All time devices developed by man have their root anchored in change. However, God does not change! "Jesus Christ the same yesterday, and today and forever" (Heb. 13:8). Therefore, to understand the *mystery of God's will* in light of His sovereignty and the free will of man, we must reflect on what was before the ordered ages and what will be after the ordered ages. There will be no time. Time will be no more. Herein lies the rest of the mystery.

What man sees is bound by time. God is not bound by time; He created time. Therefore, God stands outside of time and can see past, present, and future all at once. That is how God can with foreknowledge, elect and predestinate a believer. God knows what man will choose but does not influence man's choices. That is how God can purpose an event and ensure that it is done. That is how God can equip a prophet and bring their prophecy to exactness. That is how God's sovereignty and will can be reconciled with man's freewill.

Chapter 13

Mystery of the Seven Stars and the Seven Lampstands

Revelation 1:20

I. Context

➢ The Revelation of Jesus Christ
➢ Delivered to John as prophecy was delivered to Daniel
➢ John instructed to write in a book to the seven churches

II. The significance of Seven in time and completion (Rev. 1:20)

➢ Seven messengers for seven churches.
➢ Periods of seven applied to creation, dispensations, famines, work, healing and judgments.
➢ Seven by biblical definition infers completion.

III. The impact of the first resurrection and the promises to the Church on the mystery of the Lampstands

➢ Resurrection of Old Testament saints, Church-age saints and those who are alive (1 Thess. 4:13–17; Rev. 5:9–10).

> The Church not appointed to the wrath of God (1 Thess. 5:9; Rev. 3:10).

IV. What the Seven Golden Lampstands Represent during the Church Age (Rev. 1:20; 3:19)

> Seven locations, seven congregations.
> The spiritual state and coinciding judgment by Jesus of seven congregations.
> The future view of the Church periods throughout the Church age.

V. The interpretation of the messages and the mystery

> Seven different congregational characteristics with one dominant feature in every period.
> The believer's response in the current times.

Mystery of the Seven Stars and Seven Lampstands
Revelation 1:20

I. Context: In Revelation 1:1, the introduction of the revelation of Jesus Christ comes from the authority of the Father who gave it to Jesus, who in turn gave it to an angel who gave it to the apostle John. Why this chain of custody of the Revelation of Jesus? It was delivered to John in the same way the prophecy concerning Israel in the last days was delivered to Daniel (Dan. 9:20–23; 10:13–14). Jesus had already faced skepticism, criticism, rejection, and crucifixion led by the Jewish religious leaders because of who He was and what He had come to do. Authenticity of the prophecy given to John was to be indisputable. In John 5:36, speaking of John the Baptist the herald of the Savior, Jesus said "But I have greater witness than that of John; for the works which the Father hath given me to finish, the same works that I do bear witness of me, that the Father hath sent me." While teaching and equipping His disciples for service after His death and resurrection, Jesus revealed the Church that He would build (Matt. 16:17–18). He finished His work on the cross, when He was crucified and died that mankind might have forgiveness of sin and receive eternal life. What was revealed to John was not the continuation of Christ as Suffering Servant. That was finished. When Jesus said from the cross, "It is finished" (John 19:30), He had completed what the Father had sent Him to do. Justification was complete, salvation by grace through faith in Jesus was available to all who would believe, and Jesus had established and set the foundation for His Church that would go and share the good news.

What John is shown is the events preceding the second coming of Jesus Christ, the Lord of lords and the King of kings and what happens on this earth when Jesus returns. In revealing the coming of the King, John was instructed to write those things which he had seen, the vision, the things which are, the condition of the seven churches he was to write to, and the things which shall be hereafter, what the future would hold for an evil world and for those who would turn to Jesus as Lord and Savior (Rev. 1:19). He was to write to the seven churches that were located in Asia (Rev. 1:4).

II. The Significance of Seven in Time and Completion

In John's Patmos vision, Jesus tells John to write to seven churches, and when he turns to see the voice that spoke to him, he saw seven golden lampstands and in the middle of the lampstands was Jesus and in His right hand were seven stars (Rev. 1:9–16). The lampstands and the stars are explained in Revelation 1:20: "The mystery of the seven stars which thou sawest in my right hand, and the seven golden lampstands. The seven stars are the angels of the seven churches; and the seven lampstands which thou sawest are the seven churches." Neither the church locations or congregations were a mystery. The angels or messengers could possibly be a mystery but not likely. The history of these churches would not be a mystery. So, what is the mystery?

A review of the context of seven as it is used in various biblical events reveal much more than a number. The Greek word for seven is *hepta* (ἑπτά). The word signifies to be full and generally expresses completeness.[35] So, how would seven churches with their messengers be full or complete? There could have been letters to other churches besides the seven selected. To understand the significance of seven in scripture as it relates to completion of time periods, famines, work, healing, and judgment, seven examples are given:

> ➤ Creation: "And on the seventh day God ended his work which he had made; and he rested on the seventh day from all his work which he had made" (Gen. 2:2).

> ➤ Seven dispensations of mankind: Paul in Ephesians 1:10 gives the context of dispensationalism while writing to the Ephesians concerning their position according to grace. "That in the dispensation of the fulness of times he might gather together in one all things in Christ, both which are in heaven, and which are on earth; even in him." Dispensation is the Greek word *oikonomia* (οἰκομία), which signifies the management or stewardship of affairs.[36] God gave mankind stewardship over seven time periods to manage. They are:

>> 1. Innocence (Gen. 1:28)
>> 2. Conscience (Gen. 3:22–24)

---

[35] W.E. Vine, *Expository Dictionary of New Testament Words*.

[36] Ibid.

3. Human government: man-to-man responsibility for the shedding the blood of fellow man (Gen. 9:6)
4. Promise (Gen. 12:1–3)
5. Law (Exod. 19:5–8)
6. Grace (John 1:17)
7. Kingdom (Eph. 1:10). All things will be gathered together under the rule of Christ for a thousand years as He rules with a rod of iron on the earth (Rev. 20:1–3).

➤ Seven years of plenty and seven years of famine in Egypt when Joseph rose to prominence (Gen. 41:16–32).

➤ Sabbatical year of rest for the land as commanded by God to Israel. They were to work the land for six years and allow the land to rest the seventh year (Gen. 25).

➤ Naaman instructed by Elisha to wash in the Jordan River seven times to be healed of leprosy (2 Kings 5:10).

➤ Seventy-Sevens determined upon Israel and the holy city for ignoring the Sabbatical year (2 Chron. 36:21; Dan. 9:24).

➤ Seven years is the length of the tribulation period (Dan. 9:27; Matt. 24:21).

In each of these examples, completeness is not only implied; it is demonstrated.

All must heed Peter's warning in 2 Peter 1:20 to study prophecy in the context of all the scripture, not in isolation Therefore, if other scripture is to be used to understand the significance of the letters to the seven churches, how would the seven letters to seven churches represent completion? The answer is found in the dispensations set forth by God. The age of grace, the Church age, has a beginning and an ending. It started at Pentecost and will end when Christ raptures His church. So, is the time of the Church age divided into separate periods? Every indication is that it is with the church at Ephesus, representing the beginning, and the church at Laodicea, representing the end of the Church age. Ephesus would represent the apostolic church that ended with the death of the last apostle, John, and the church at Laodicea would represent the end of the Church age with a lukewarm, apathetic congregation that will have little influence on a world that is about to enter into great tribulation.

III. The Impact of the First Resurrection and the Promises to the Church on the Mystery of the Lampstands: The question by so many for so long has been: will the Church be subjected to the great tribulation or will the Church age end prior to the tribulation? The following scriptures support the Church age ending prior to the tribulation:

1. Concerning the resurrection in 1 Corinthians 15:51, Paul said, "Behold I shew you a mystery; We shall not all sleep. But we shall be changed, In a moment, in the twinkling of an eye, at the last trump: for the trumpet shall sound, and the dead shall be raised incorruptible and we shall be changed." Those dead raised and those alive changed.

2. When? "For the Lord himself shall descend from heaven with a shout with the voice of the archangel, and with the trump of God: and the dead in Christ shall rise first: Then we which are alive and remain shall be caught up together with them in the clouds, to meet the Lord in the air: and so shall we ever be with the Lord" (1 Thess. 4:16–17).

3. The Church will be caught up to meet Jesus in the air, not appointed to God's wrath during the tribulation. "For God hath

not appointed us to wrath, but to obtain salvation by our Lord Jesus Christ" (1 Thess. 5:9).

4. In every letter to the seven churches, Jesus is seen judging the churches but not condemning the churches to absolute misery. In fact, the promise to the church at Philadelphia was: "Because thou hast kept the word of my patience, I also will keep thee from the hour of temptation, which shall come upon all the world, to try them that dwell upon the earth" (Rev. 3:10).

IV. What the Seven Golden Lampstands Represent During the Church Age [37]

If the seven churches and the messages applied to them represent time periods within the Church age, a logical breakdown would look like the following:

1. The Apostolic Church AD 68–100, represented by Ephesus: the apostolic authority within the Church ended when the last apostle John died around AD 100.

2. The Martyr Church AD 100–313, represented by Smyrna: The persecution of Christians diminished when the Roman Empire legalized Christianity under Emperor Constantine in AD 313.

3. The Compromising Church AD 414–590, represented by Pergamum: During this period influence from multiple directions and the lack of access to the written Word promoted an environment of compromise and dilution of the Word.

---

[37] Tommy L. Jamison, *Revelation for the Layperson*.

4. The Corrupted Church, The Crusades (1095–1492) AD 590–1500, represented by Thyatira: During the time the Church was ruled by the Pope, the Crusades raged, promises of forgiveness of sins by the priest, called indulgences, was used as a recruiting tool. Papal authority went unchecked. Worship of the Virgin Mary and the doctrine of purgatory were fundamental teachings. The environment changed when Martin Luther questioned the doctrines and nailed his 95 Theses (Disputation on the Power and Efficacy of Indulgences) on the door of the Wittenberg Castle Church in Germany on October 31, 1517. The Protestant Reformation had begun.

5. The Feeble Church, A remnant Church (The Protestant Reformation (1517–1800), represented by Sardis: Beginning as a fledging feeble group, persecuted by the Catholic Church, it moved throughout Europe and America.

6. The Revived Church, the Professing Church, the Faithful Church (1800–?), represented by Philadelphia: Many great revivals have been experienced all over the world since the early 1800s, with millions coming to know Christ as Lord and Savior. Revivals preached by Jeremiah Lanphier, D.L. Moody, Billy Sunday, Bill Bright, Billy Graham, and many others drew men to the truth of the Word of God and their need for a savior. Has this dominant time ended?

7. The Lukewarm Church, represented by Laodicea: Is this the Church today?

V. The Interpretation of the Messages and the Mystery:

So, how should the interpretation of the message to the seven churches be viewed? First, these are messages to specific congregations that existed in John's day. John had served at some of these churches. Second, this should be viewed as messages to churches throughout the Church age. Third, history would show the condition of the churches John is addressing to coincide with the vitality and profile of churches from the early churches in Acts until now. The chronology would begin with the church at Ephesus, which was the apostolic church, and end with the church at Laodicea, the apathetic church.

The approach to understanding each of the letters is first to view the posture of the Lord Jesus as He examines the churches. Second, review what the church has been doing, where they are obedient, where they fall short, and what they need to correct. Third, the consequences of not responding to the Lord's instructions reveals His judgment. None of the judgments of the Lord Jesus indicates He will thrust His bride, the Church, into the great tribulation. The sum of the mystery is: at any given time during the Church age, there will be churches demonstrating every characteristic of the seven churches John is told to write. However, at the same time, there will be a dominant position of the majority of churches that will be as one of the seven churches John is writing. The Church age is well into, if not past, being a revived, faithful church. Is the Church age moving toward completion with the dominant Church position that of lukewarmness, and apathy? The believer is to watch, watch, watch, and not be paralyzed with current events but be faithful and obedient in sharing the gospel of grace while there is still time.

Chapter 14

Mystery, Babylon the Great, the Mother of Harlots and Abominations of the Earth

Revelation 17:5

I.   **Context (Rev. 17:1–2)**

> ➤ The angel with the seven bowls.
> ➤ The harlot sitting on many waters

II. **Events that precede the judgment of the Harlot**

> ➤ Great tribulation prophesied by Daniel and Jesus. (Matt. 24; Dan. 7:24–28).
> ➤ Babylon the harlot, and Babylon the political and commercial institutions (Rev. 17, 18).

III. **Mysteries that identify the sequence of events**

> ➤ The mystery of the Gospel. (Eph. 6:19) The Gospel of the kingdom preached during the tribulation by the 144,000 sealed Jews (Matt. 24:14; Rev. 7).

➢ The mystery of the resurrection (1 Cor. 1551). The Church is raptured, caught up in the air.

➢ The mystery of the seven stars and seven golden lampstands (Rev. 1:20). The Church age ends prior to the tribulation.

IV. What does the Harlot represent? (Rev. 17:2–4)

➢ The adornment of the harlot. Dressed as religious Israel, the harlot (Ezek. 16:2–41).
➢ The activity of the harlot, committing fornication with the kings of the earth as Israel did (Jer. 2:20; 3:1–8).
➢ The cup of the harlot, full of abominations (Rev. 17:4–5).

1. Sexual abominations.
2. Spiritual abominations.
3. Social abominations.

➢ The cup full of the filthiness of fornication (Rev. 17:4).

V. What is the relationship between the harlot and the Beast; Convenience and Treachery?

➢ The beast is both a man and a kingdom (Rev. 11:7; Rev. 13, 14).
➢ The harlot will martyr many Jewish and Gentile believers (Rev. 17:6).
➢ The harlot is destroyed, and the beast and Satan are worshiped (Rev. 13:4; 17:8, 16).
➢ Jesus overcomes and casts the beast and Satan into the lake of fire (Rev. 17:14; 19:20; 20:10).

Mystery, Babylon the Great, the Mother of Harlots and
Abominations of the Earth
Revelation 17:5

I. Context: In Revelation 17, John is shown by one of the angels with the seven bowls the judgment of the mother of harlots. In verse 5 the woman is identified by the name written on her forehead as "MYSTERY, BABYLON THE GREAT, THE MOTHER OF HARLOTS AND ABOMINATIONSTIONS OF THE EARTH." In verse 15, the harlot is described as one that sits upon many waters, which means that she has dominance over many people, nations, and tongues. In verse 18, the angel further identifies the woman as that great city Babylon which reigns over the kings of the earth. So, what does this harlot represent, and how will the judgment take place?

II. Events that Precede the Judgment of the Harlot: In Matthew 24, Jesus warned His disciples that catastrophic events would take place on the earth prior to His return to establish His kingdom. He told His disciples in verse 21 that there would be great tribulation such as was not since the beginning of the world to this time, no, or ever shall be. Daniel was given understanding of the time of the great tribulation in Daniel 7:24–28, and John was shown how the events of the tribulation would unfold, including the judgment of the ancient city of Babylon in Revelation 17 and 18. The judgment of all that the ancient city of Babylon represented; religious, political, and commercial, would be judged. What is different from the destruction of Babylon the harlot and Babylon the political and commercial center is the harlot is a mystery where the other designations are not. That is what separates Revelation 17 from Revelation 18 in context and content. Political institutions come and go, and are not a mystery. Commercial institutions, currency, and governments come and go and are not a mystery. However, Mystery, Babylon the Great, the Mother of Harlots and Abominations of the Earth is different and is a mystery of great interest.

Using the mystery of the gospel, the mystery of the resurrection, and the mystery of the seven stars and seven golden lampstands, a sequence of events can be identified that will place the harlot's activity and destruction in the context and time of the great tribulation. They are:

1. The gospel of the kingdom is the beginning of the mystery of the gospel and was preached by John the Baptist, Jesus, and His disciples. The message was repent and believe the gospel. The gospel of the kingdom ceased to be preached when Jesus the Messiah was rejected and crucified.

2. When Jesus was crucified and was raised from the dead, He gave His disciples the great commission to go to all nations, baptizing them in the name of the Father, the Son, and the Holy Spirit, teaching them to observe all things that Jesus had commanded. They were to go forth preaching the Gospel of grace that began at Pentecost. The preaching of the Gospel of grace will end when the Church is raptured to meet Jesus in the air.

3. When the Church is taken from the earth as indicated by the mystery of the resurrection and the mystery of the seven stars and seven golden lampstands, the Gospel of the kingdom will again be preached by the 144,000 Jews, 12,000 from each tribe, during the tribulation.

4. The 144,000 Jews that are sealed to again preach repentance and believe the Gospel of Christ will not proceed without great opposition. The opposition will come from an apostate religion, sponsored by international leadership. This is where "Mystery,

Babylon the Great, the Mother of Hariots And Abominations of the Earth" comes to the forefront.

III. What Does the Harlot Represent? The clothing, jewelry, and the cup of the harlot are the primary indicators of what the harlot represents. Again. Peter's words of warning concerning prophecy is timely: "Knowing this first, that no prophecy of the scripture is of any private interpretation" (2 Pet. 1:20). John was shown how the harlot was clothed. She was arrayed in purple and scarlet color and bedecked with gold and precious stones and pearls, having a golden cup in her hand, full of abominations of filthiness of her fornication. She had committed fornication with the kings of the earth. A look for this type of attire in other scripture gives the key. In Ezekiel 16:2–41, the picture of a religious whore is described. The religious whore is Israel. She is adorned with fine clothes and jewelry, and she has played the whore with Egypt, Assyria, and Chaldea. As Assyria destroyed the northern kingdom and Babylon (Chaldea) destroyed the southern kingdom, so will the kings of the earth in Revelation 17:16 destroy the mother of harlots. With Israel depicted as a religious whore by Ezekiel and Jeremiah (Jer. 2:20; 3:1–8), there is no question the harlot represents a world-wide religion.

The contents of the cup the harlot is holding (Rev. 17:4) gives further evidence that the harlot represents apostate religion and just how vile the religion becomes. The Greek word for abomination is *bdelugma*: meaning an object of disgust, primarily associated with constant acts of idolatry. The Old Testament gives the laundry list of abominations that God warned against. They are:

1. Sexual abominations: homosexuality, incest, lewdness, whoredom, and sodomy (Deut. 23:18, Lev. 18:22–26, Ezek. 16:43,20:30).

2. Spiritual abominations: idolatry, divination, enchanter, consultor of mediums, and witchcraft (Deut. 13:14, 18:12).

3. Social abominations: lying lips, cheating, and stealing (Prov. 11:1; 12:22).

Filthiness is also contained in the harlot's cup, describing her lewdness and moral impurity (Ezek. 24:13).

IV. Who is the Harlot? When looking at the timing of the Harlot coming on the scene with great power and influence over the nations, it is highly unlikely the religious whore will spring up and be that dominant in three and a half years, but that is the longevity for the harlot because she will be destroyed by the beast and the kings of the earth paving the way for the worship of the beast in the second half of the tribulation. That means much of the foundation of apostate religion will be put in place prior to the beginning of the tribulation. This should come as no surprise as the acceptance by so-called Christian denominations of openly sexual abominations, idolatry, child sacrifice, and many other forms of filth as part of their doctrine.

With many Christian denominations allowing the leaven of the world to permeate their beliefs and values, it is unlikely the power and tenacity to establish such a broad-based religion will come from the offspring of a lukewarm church as Laodicea. It will come from an established religion that will be brutal, including death toward the saints. John understood this to be true when he said, "I saw the woman drunk with the blood of the saints, and with blood of the martyrs of Jesus; and when I saw her, I wondered with great wonder" (Rev. 17:6). Apostate Christendom will stand for nothing, yet will believe anything. Those in that category will be as they are today; just get along and go along.

So, is there a dominant religion today that is intolerant of any who are not part of their religion? Is there a dominant religion today whose followers target Christians and Jews to murder, even if it takes killing themselves to kill a Jew or Christian? Is there a dominant religion today where there is no separation of the religion from the government that supports it? Is there a dominant religion today that views the religious leader to also be the national leader? The answer is yes! What is that religion?

V. What is the Relationship Between the Harlot and the Beast? Just as the harlot is an institution of man energized by Satan, so is the beast both a kingdom and a man energized by Satan. John had already been given insight into this beast who ascended out of the bottomless pit to make war against the two witnesses and was allowed to kill them (Rev. 11:7). The Beast with seven heads is a matter of location. The seven heads are seven mountains or hills of Rome and the ten horns were kingdoms both confirmed in chapter 14, and Revelation 13. Also confirmed in chapter 14 is that the beast is both a kingdom and a person. The kingdom is the old Roman Empire and the beast is the leader of the reconstituted nations of Europe that made up the old empire. The idea that something "was and is not and yet is" signifies existence, dormancy, or death and reconstitution or resurrection. This is what happened to both the beast, a nation, and the beast, a person. The beast, the person, is no doubt the Man of Sin, the Antichrist, and the puppet of Satan. He receives a deadly wound (Rev.13:3) but the wound is healed (Rev. 13:12). Therefore, *he was*, then he received a deadly wound and *is not*, then he ascended out of the abyss, *yet is.* The nation of Rome *was* in John's day, *is not* in our day and *yet is* or will be during the tribulation.

How would a religion and government leadership become so intertwined that they are seen as unity? That question is answered by John as he records the image of the harlot and the beast she is riding. What has the beast been doing? The beast, the man of sin who heads the old Roman Empire, has been consolidating power for three and half years as revealed in Revelation 6:2 and Daniel 8:25. The beast has been blaspheming God and making war with the saints (Rev. 13:5–7). This would be consistent with nations of today headed by a religious leader who embraces a god rooted in the Old Testament but not the Lord Jesus Christ and not the God of Abraham, Isaac, and Jacob. The beast, along with the government he controls, will covenant with an established religion, the harlot, to persecute Christians and gain power. Ultimately the motive of the beast is to mandate worship of himself by the world (Rev. 13:8). The harlot will use the beast to help mandate a worldwide religion (Rev. 17:6, 15), and while the religious leaders of the harlot and their followers think they are in control, they quickly learn it is Satan who is pulling all the strings. Once the beast has gained total power over the earth and is viewed as a god (Rev. 13:4), he with his subordinate kings will destroy the harlot (Rev. 17:16–17).

All along, Satan has coveted the position of God, and through his manipulation of apostate religion and the power he gives the beast and the false prophet, Satan the dragon will be worshiped by the world (Rev. 13:4; 17:8). Although Satan, the beast and the kings of the earth will destroy apostate religion so that Satan himself will be worshiped, it does not end there. God will judge those who worship the beast and Satan and cast them and the false trinity (Satan, the beast, and the false prophet) into the lake of fire (Rev. 19:20; 20:10).

Something to ponder: What is the religion that teaches hatred and murder of Jews and Christians? What is the religion that teaches that the nations' leadership should only be of the same religious faith? What is the religion whose national leaders are ordained as their spiritual leaders? What is the religion that desires dominance over the modern city of Rome?

Chapter 15

The Mystery of God Should Be Finished and the Mystery of the Wisdom of God

Revelation 10:7; 1 Corinthians 2:7–8

I. **Context: The Mystery of God Should Be Finished and The Mystery of the Wisdom of God to bring all to completion**

➢ The little book John is instructed to eat (Rev. 10:1–7).

    1. Jeremiah was instructed to eat the Word of God (Jer. 15:16).
    2. Ezekiel was instructed to eat the Word of God (Ezekiel 3:1–4).
    3. All contained the prophecy revealed by God.

➢ To finish implies a beginning.

    1. Starting with the beginning of time.
    2. Moving through history as the deep things of God are revealed by the Holy Spirit to the believer.

II. **The finished mystery of God purposed through The Mystery of the wisdom of God (1 Cor. 2:6–8).**

➢ Not the wisdom of the world (v. 6–7).

- ➤ The wisdom of God a hidden mystery from Satan and all intelligent creation (v. 8).
- ➤ The deep things of God revealed to the spiritually mature by the Holy Spirit (1 Cor. 2:10–14; 3:1–2).

III. The Creation is the beginning of the believer's understanding of the Mystery of God.

- ➤ God all-in-all when He created the heaven and earth (Gen. 1:1–2).
- ➤ Christ at the center of the creation (Col. 1:15–17).
- ➤ The visible creation leaves man without excuse (Rom. 1:20).
- ➤ The Trinity of God and the unique trinity of man (Gen. 1:26).

IV. The Separation of man from God due to Sin and the Provisions God made for man.

- ➤ Natural man's perception of creation, a carnal explanation of the mystery (Rom. 1:23–25).
- ➤ God's provision for Adam and Eve after their sin (Gen. 3:21).
- ➤ Cain rejected God's provision and went out from God's presence (Gen. 4:16).
- ➤ God would destroy all of civilization as man totally rejected God (Gen. 6:5–7).
- ➤ God made provision for Noah and his family as they found grace (Gen. 6:8).
- ➤ God made provision for Abraham. Faith counted for righteousness (Gen. 15:6, Rom. 4:3).
- ➤ God defines disobedience by the given law to move man to the provision of His grace through faith (Rom. 3:31–4:8).

V. The hope of man provided by the sacrifice of Christ: God's plan of redemption finished.

➢ Faith and hope in Christ or faith in something else (Rom. 8:24–25).
➢ God's plan of restoration of man was from the beginning (Gen. 3:15; John 3:16).
➢ God specifically revealed his plan of redemption for man:

1. A child born who is mighty God (Isa. 9:6–7).
2. That child, Jesus Christ, despised and rejected by the world (Isa. 53:3).
3. Jesus Christ would be beaten, abused, and crucified for our sins (Isa. 50:6; 52:13–15).
4. Jesus Christ would bear the iniquity of all mankind (Isa. 53:11).

➢ Redemption complete: "It is finished" (John 19:30).

VI. With redemption complete, what is left to finish the Mystery of God?

➢ What the mystery of God has provided in the past:

1. His sin sacrifice for man is complete.
2. His Word is complete (John1:14).
3. Man's choice is clear and concise (John 3:16; Rom. 10:9–10).
4. His Church is commissioned (Matt. 28:19–20).
5. We are told to *watch* for the things that will project the end (Mark 13:34, 35, 37).

➢ The prelude to the mystery of God finished

1. The beginning of sorrows (Matt. 24:5–12).
2. Increased evil. (2 Thess. 2:3,7).
3. Ignorant scoffers (2 Pet. 3:2–7).

> ➢ The interim of the mystery of God finished: rapture through the time of the great white throne Judgment.

VII. The Completion of the Mystery of God Finished: (1 Cor. 15:24–28)

> ➢ The end comes, and the kingdom of God is delivered up (v. 24).
> ➢ All enemies are crushed (vv. 25–26).
> ➢ God is all-in-all.

The Mystery of God Should Be Finished and the Mystery of the Wisdom of God
Revelation 10:7; 1 Corinthians 2:7–8

I. Context: In Revelation 10, John sees an angel come down from heaven with a little book in his hand. The book is open, indicating the contents are to be revealed to John. The angel lifts up his hand to heaven and swears by the God of creation that there should be time no longer, "But in the days of the voice of the seventh angel, when he shall begin to sound, *the mystery of God should be finished*, as he hath declared to his servants the prophets" (v. 7). A voice from heaven (Jesus) instructs John to take the little book and eat it. This signifying that John is to receive the Word of God. Other prophets experienced the same: Jeremiah 15:16 wrote: "Thy words were found and I did eat them, and thy word was unto me the joy and rejoicing of mine heart: for I am called by thy name, O LORD God of hosts." Also, in Ezekiel 3:1–4, Ezekiel is instructed by God to eat a scroll and go to the house of Israel and speak God's words. In Revelation 10:11, John is also instructed to prophesy again before many peoples and nations, and tongues, and kings that the mystery of God should be finished. The little book contained the remaining prophecy that God would reveal to mankind. The little book contained the rest of *the mystery of God.*

To grasp the finished mystery of God would indicate an understanding of the beginning and continued revelation of the mystery of God. That would include the things of God from the beginning of time as revealed by God and received by man through the prophets and the final prophecy revealed to John in the little book. Although the prophecy is given, that does not mean man can understand it. Only the believer through the power of the Holy Spirit is capable of understanding the things of God. Jesus made this truth clear when speaking to His disciples in John 14:25–26: "These things have I spoken unto you, Being present with you. But the Comforter, who is the Holy Spirit, whom the Father will send in my name, he shall teach you all things. And bring all things to your remembrance, whatever I have said unto you." To know *start to finish* of God's plan and purpose of redemption of mankind is to know the deep things of God.

II. The Finished Mystery of God Purposed Through The Mystery of the Wisdom of God

Just as the mysteries of Christ and the Church cannot be studied in isolation, neither can the finished mystery of God and the mystery of His wisdom. To speak of the mystery of God is to focus on the wisdom of God. By His wisdom, God planned, purposed, and revealed so much to the believer. In 1 Corinthians 2:6–8, the believer is given a glimpse into the wisdom of God that aids in the understanding of all biblical mysteries and how they will be finished:

> "Howbeit we speak wisdom among them that are perfect; (mature) yet not the wisdom of this world, nor of the princes of this world, that come to naught; But we speak the *wisdom of God in a mystery*, even the hidden wisdom, which God ordained before the world unto our glory; Which none of the princes of this world

knew: for had they known it, they would not have crucified the Lord of glory."

Had the princes of this world knew the mysteries of God, all of history would have been altered. According to Jesus's words in John
12:31,14:30, and 16:11, the chief prince of this world is Satan. Had
Satan known for sure from the beginning what the consequences
of his rebellion would be, Paul is saying he would not have orches-
trated the crucifixion. Of course, this goes back to the mystery of God's
will and the fact that He gave both angelic beings and mankind the
freedom to choose. Choices are made without necessarily knowing
the outcome and what future consequences may lie in wait. That is
why faith in God is so important. Had God revealed all to those He
created, there would be no need for faith. That is also why without
faith, it is impossible to please God (Heb. 11:6).

The "mystery of God finished" is illustrated by His infinite wisdom.
God's infinite wisdom is a mystery and can only be understood by man
through the indwelling Holy Spirit. "But God hath revealed them unto
us by his Spirit: for the Spirit searcheth all things yea, the deep things
of God." (1 Cor. 2:10). The deep things of God are all of the mysteries
He has revealed and more. They are only revealed to those who are
spiritually mature, not natural man (1 Cor. 2:14) and not those feeding
on the milk of the Word but those who desire and eat the meat of the
Word, just as John was instructed to eat the little book (1 Cor. 3:1–2).

III. The Creation is the Beginning of the Believer's Understanding of the Mystery of God as He is All-In-All in the Godhead: Father, Son, and Holy Spirit

"In the beginning God created the heaven and the earth and the earth
was without form, and void; and darkness was upon the face of the
deep. And the Spirit of God moved upon the face of the waters" (Gen.

1:1–2). At this time, the fullness of the Godhead was revealed through Christ Jesus to man. "Who is the image of the invisible God, the first-born of every creature: For by him were all things created, that are in heaven, and that are in earth, visible and invisible whether they be thrones, or dominions, or principalities, or powers all things were created by him, and for him: and he is before all things, and by him all things consist" (Col. 1:15–17). The scripture clearly reveals the fullness of the Godhead: Father, Son, and Holy Spirit. The scripture also indicates God to be all-in-all at the time of His creation. What is not revealed to man is when God created the heavenly host. We do not know when Satan and the other angels were created. What man does know is the eternal Godhead was clearly seen by Satan, and he with a third of the angels rebelled against God. Also, God has revealed Himself through the creation, and man is without excuse when it comes to how all things came into being (Rom. 1:20).

When "God said, let us make man in our image" (Gen. 1:26), He clearly revealed that man is more than flesh. Man is unique among God's creation. As God is a trinity, so is man in the image of God: body, soul, spirit. Adam and Eve were created with a body, a soul, and a spirit. However, all things changed with their body when they sinned. Their soul remained, their spirit died and their body would eventually die. All in Adam are born with a body and soul, but are spiritually dead. "Even when we were dead in sins hath quickened us together with Christ, (by grace ye are saved)" (Eph. 2:5). Without salvation by grace through faith in the Lord Jesus, man is eternally separated from God.

IV. The Separation of Man from God Due to Sin and the Provisions God Made for Man: As the creation remains a mystery to the natural man who attempts to ascribe God's work to other gods, to chance (Big Bang), and to evolution, sin has continued to rule and reign over man (Rom. 1:23–25). As a result of disobedience, man lost dominion over the earth that God created (Gen. 1:26). However, before God created man, He knew man would choose to separate himself from God. God knew what Adam and Eve would do, as God made provision with a blood sacrifice for them when He slew animals and took their skin for a covering that they might be fit for the presence of God and not remain separated (Gen. 3:21). This was not an afterthought by God, but the first step in removing the separation due to disobedience and sin. God knew most of mankind would choose to go their own way and reject the one who created them. Cain, in anger, would kill Abel. God knew Cain would choose to go out from the presence of the Lord and choose a life of wandering and misery rather than repent. (Gen. 4:16). God knew mankind would become so evil that He would eventually destroy them, except for Noah and his family. (Gen. 6:5–8)

Even after the flood, God knew man would have a short memory of the worldwide destruction by the flood and would follow the same path of sin and separation. Before God would provide guidance by His law, He would show that righteousness before Him would require faith: "For what saith the scripture? Abraham believed God, and it was counted unto him for righteousness." (Rom. 4:3, Gen. 15:6). Justification by faith was always the means of being counted righteous before God. Adam and Eve did not trust God to be truthful and believed Satan. Cain did not bring an acceptable offering to God in faith. The whole pre-flood civilization did not believe God and rejected the preaching of Noah; for their unbelief and gross iniquity, God would destroy them.

God would eventually provide the law to show mankind what con-stituted sin and its consequences. God, through His law, would show man that he was not capable of meeting the requirements of the law and that he must turn to God in faith or remain eternally separated from His presence.

V. The Hope of Man Provided by the Sacrifice of Christ: God's Plan of Redemption Finished: Throughout the ages, man has questioned his origin and his destination. Man can study all of recorded history, dig deep into the sciences as to the age of the universe, and attempt by hypothesis and conjecture to explain why he is here and where he is going. However, when all is said and done, man is left with choices based on faith, either believe and trust the God of creation or have faith in something else. Even an atheist must have great faith. This is part of the mystery of God. God will show us much but will never eliminate the requirement for faith in Him. Paul made this clear in Romans 8:24–25: "For we are saved by hope: but hope that is seen is not hope: for what a man seeth why doth he yet hope for? But if we hope for that we see not, then do we with patience wait for it." That hope is salvation by grace through faith in the Lord Jesus Christ. There is nothing we can do to earn salvation (Eph. 2:8).

God, from the beginning, has provided that hope and reached out to man to redeem and restore him. God spoke of crushing sin by His coming in the person of Jesus Christ in the flesh when He cursed the serpent and put enmity between the serpent and woman (Gen. 3:14–25). God would show just how much He loved and desired to restore mankind to fellowship with Himself by paying man's sin debt. "For God so loved the world that he gave his only begotten Son, that whosoever believeth in him should not perish but have everlasting life" (John 3:16). Threaded throughout the Bible is the message of the good news of God's plan of salvation and restoration of man. Isaiah spoke of the coming Savior, Christ the Lord, in Isaiah 9:6–7: "For unto us a child is born, unto us a son is given, and the government shall be upon his shoulder; and his name shall be called Wonderful, Counselor, The Mighty God, The Everlasting Father, The Prince of Peace." God told us He would be despised and rejected by man (Isa. 53:3), that He would be abused and beaten so badly that He would not be recognizable (Isa. 50:6; 52:13–15), and God told us the Savior's soul would be sacrificed for the sins of man (Isa. 53:10). All that God did to send the Savior who would justify many by bearing the iniquity of many (Isa. 53:11) is all part of the mystery of God. Why would He go to the cross for sinful man? Why would God put so much effort into justifying and restoring sinful man? Jesus said from the cross, "It is finished" (John 19:30). That is all part of the mystery of God and His wisdom!

VI. With Redemption Complete, What Is Left to be Finished? What God has provided man is His Word. In His Word, God gave man the sequence of the creation. God gave man the instructions from the garden to the law for obedience, and when man disobeyed God, He made early provision for restoration. God has shown there is a limit as to how long He will strive with man before He will judge him. God showed man that justification comes by faith in Him. God gave the Law to show man he cannot meet God's requirements for righteousness by his works. Finally, the Word came in the flesh "And the Word was made flesh, and dwelt among us (and we beheld his glory, the glory as of the only begotten of the father), full of grace and truth" (John 1:14). By the birth, life, death, resurrection, and ascension of the Savior, Christ the Lord, God provided a clear and concise choice of redemption (John 3:16; Rom. 10:9–10). God established His Church to go into all the world teaching the gospel of grace and baptizing believers in the name of the Father, Son, and Holy Spirit. But, when the iniquity of man becomes full again, God will finish His mystery.

Jesus told us to watch, watch and watch for the mystery to be finished. Jesus said in Mark 13:32, "But of that day and that hour knoweth no man, no, not the angels who are in heaven, neither the Son, but the Father. Take heed, watch and pray; for ye know not when the time is." Again, in Mark 13: 34, 35, and 37, Jesus said to *watch*. The believer is to watch for the signs that will indicate the beginning of the end.

The prelude to the mystery of God finished is the beginning of sorrows that Jesus spoke of in Matthew 24:8, "All these are the beginning of sorrows." What are they? (Matt. 24:4–14).

1. Deception by false Christ (v. 5).
2. Wars and rumors of wars (v. 6).
3. Famines (v. 7).
4. Pestilence (v. 7).
5. Earthquakes (v. 7).
6. Lawlessness; iniquity will abound (v. 12).
7. Falling away (2 Thess. 2:3).
8. Ignorant scoffer. (2 Pet. 3:2–7).
9. Increased knowledge but not coming to the truth (2 Tim. 3:1–7).

The interim of the mystery of God finished is:

1. Holy Spirit taken out of the way and lawlessness increases (2 Thess. 2:7).
2. The rapture of the Church (1 Cor. 15:51–52; 1 Thess. 4:13; 5:11; Rev. 1:20; 3:20).
3. The tribulation period with the Seal, Trumpet and Bowl Judgments spelled out in Revelation 4–16, as Jesus foretold in Matthew 24:21.
4. The man of sin revealed, the son of perdition (2 Thess. 2:3).
5. The preaching in all the world of the Gospel of the Kingdom by the 144,000 Jews (Matt. 24:14, R. 7; and the preaching of the everlasting Gospel by an angel; Rev. 14:6).
6. The Battle of Armageddon, the Marriage of the Lamb to His bride, the Church, and the second coming of Christ (Rev. 19).
7. The thousand-year reign of Christ, with Satan bound in the abyss (Rev. 20).
8. Satan released to tempt the nations and is defeated and cast into the lake of fire (Rev. 20:10).
9. The great white throne judgment of the second resurrection unto damnation (John 5:29; Rev. 20:11–15).

VII. The Completion of the Mystery of God Finished. In 1 Corinthians 15:24–28, Paul was led by the Holy Spirit to show the believer the completion of the mystery of God.

> "Then cometh the end, when he shall have delivered up the kingdom to God, even the father when he shall have put down all rule and all authority and power. For he must reign till he hath put all enemies under his feet. The last enemy that shall be destroyed is death. For he hath put all things under his feet. But when he saith all things are put under him, it is manifest that he is excepted who did put all things under him. And when all things shall be subdued unto him, then shall the Son also himself be subject unto him that put all things under him, that God may bel all in all."

As Jesus pointed to the beginning of sorrows, He instructed John to point to the end of sorrows (Rev. 21:4). The end of sorrows will happen when Jesus has delivered up the kingdom of God to the Father and God will be all in all.

The Lord shows the believer the eternal state in Revelation 21–22. As man will be a trinity in one spirit, soul and glorified body, so, will God be all in all Father, Son, and Holy Spirit. The believer in the eternal state will not worship the Father and Son as separate personalities of the Godhead because man will see God all-in-all. This is the completion of the mystery of God.

Epilogue

The epilogue to the mysteries revealed by God is not a summary and in no way intended to convey the full explanations presented for each. Although each mystery can be studied independently, the epilogue provides enough information to allow the reader to call to mind the significance and relative order of each mystery as they apply to other biblical studies. The ability to reflect on the mysteries in the context of all of God's Word will help the believer who desires the meat of the Word and to know the deep things of God become a better minister and steward of the mysteries.

I.   The Mystery of Christ (Col. 4:3, Colossians 1:24–29)

Christ the Messiah was not hidden from the sons of men. Isaiah gave a full account of the coming of the Suffering Servant and Mighty God. Christ indwelling the individual believer during the Church age was the mystery. The Spirit of Christ (the Holy Spirit) indwelling the believer came in power first at Pentecost and will continue until the Church is taken out of this world (the Rapture).

II.   The Mystery of Israel's Blindness. (Rom. 11:25).

What is Israel's spiritual blindness is the Gentiles' spiritual blessing. God chose Israel because of His covenant with Abraham, Isaac, and Jacob whom He loved and desired they become a nation of priest. Because of Israel's continued disobedience and rebellion against God's law, their idolatry, whoredom with other nations, and final rejection of the Messiah, God pronounced judgment that caused Israel to be blind and deaf to His plan of redemption through His Son. Jesus first went to his own (the Jews), but his own did not receive Him. Therefore, the Gospel was taken to the Gentiles through the apostle Paul. The presentation of the Gospel was then channeled through the Church of which Christ established as the Jews rejected the kingdom that was at hand. The Church was commissioned to go and share the Gospel.

The spiritual blindness will last through the Church age but will come to an end during the tribulation. During the seven years of tribulation and into the millennial reign, Israel will be saved as a nation. Their blindness will turn to mourning as they look upon the one they pierced (Zech. 12:10).

III. The Mystery of the Church (Eph. 3:1–12; Col. 1:24–27)

The Church was not revealed to either Old Testament saint (prophet, priest, believer) or angel (good, bad, Satan). None saw it coming. This is the wisdom of God. The body of Christ composed of both Jews and Gentiles is the mystery. Israel will not fully understand this until the millennial reign when some Jews will be of the bride of Christ and others will be friends of the Bridegroom (Messiah).

IV. The Mystery of Christ and the Church (Eph. 5:32)

Christ and the Church are depicted in a marriage relationship that is unique, exclusive, and subject to the will of God. This is a spiritual marriage illustrated by an earthly marriage between believers. The spiritual marriage shows Christ's love and commitment for his bride, the Church. That commitment includes the sacrifice of His soul that He might redeem His bride.

V. The Mystery of the Resurrection (1 Cor. 15:51)

Jesus pointed to two types of resurrections; the resurrection of life and the resurrection of damnation. The first fruit of the resurrection of life was Jesus, followed by some Old Testament saints who rose after the resurrection of Jesus and walked among many in the city of Jerusalem. The next event of the resurrection of life will be most Old Testament saints and the Church saints who have died. Immediately, in the twinkling of an eye, those of the Church who are living at the time will be changed and caught up to be with Jesus in the air, receiving a glorified body. They do not die but are raptured before the tribulation begins. At the end of the tribulation, those who have turned to Jesus and died or were martyred will also be resurrected. The last resurrection or the resurrection of damnation will occur at the end of the thousand-year reign of Christ. Those raised will face the great white throne judgement, a judgement of damnation.

VI. The Mystery of the Gospel (Eph. 6:19)

This is not speaking of the four gospels according to Matthew, Mark, Luke, and John. The Gospel mystery is dispensational, starting with the Gospel of the kingdom, followed by the Gospel of grace and the Gospel of Paul. During the tribulation period, the Gospel of the kingdom will again be preached by the 144,000 sealed Jews, followed by an angel that will preach the everlasting gospel.

VII. The Mystery of Faith (1 Tim. 3:9)

Jesus is the author and finisher of our faith. Where Jesus defines and exemplifies faith by His life and death for the sins of the world, Satan is faithless because he witnessed the substance and evidence of the glory, majesty, and power of God and thought he could be like the Most High. Here lies the two extremes of faith, and mankind is somewhere between the two. For mankind, first there is saving faith, then comes living faith, maturing faith, and dying faith. The believer's faith is a walk-through life and should follow the example of Jesus in obedience and hope.

VIII. The Mystery of Godliness (1 Tim. 3:16)

By nature, man is not godly. Godliness is defined and exemplified by the life and death of the Lord Jesus Christ for the atonement of mankind's sins. The believer is to practice godliness, with Jesus as the only example in their behavior in vocation, before other believers, before unbelievers, and before God in all humility.

IX. The Mystery of Iniquity (2 Thess. 2:7)

Iniquity was conceived by Satan, believed by mankind, imputed by the law, hindered by the Holy Spirit, and will progressively get worse with the implementation of man's values and laws. Iniquity will reach its fullness when the Holy Spirit ceases to hinder. With the giving of the law, God will judge presumptuous sin more harshly than sin in ignorance. Satan started it, yet, God, at the end of the thousand-year reign, will end it, culminating in the great white throne judgment of Christ.

X. The Mystery of the Kingdom of God (Mark 4:11; Luke 8:10).

The domain of God's kingdom includes all of creation. That domain includes angels, good and bad, Satan, all of mankind, every intelligent being. That is what God rules over. However, only those who are willing to be subject to the will of God are *in* the kingdom of God. To enter the kingdom of God, a person must be born spiritually. It is spiritual.

XI. *The Mysteries of the Kingdom of Heaven (Matt. 13:11).*

The culmination of the promise and covenant with King David that his kingdom and throne would last forever came through Jesus Christ. It is dispensational, and the full display will take place during the thousand-year reign of Christ on earth and last forever when it is merged into the kingdom of God in the eternal state. Both believers and unbelievers will occupy the domain in the Church age and the earthly reign of Christ but will be purged of the unbelievers at the end of the thousand-year reign to enter into the kingdom of God. The kingdom of heaven is earthly and of the flesh.

XII. *The Mystery of God's Will (Eph. 1:9)*

The mystery of God's will reveals the relationship of God's sovereignty to the free will of man. The reconciliation of adoption, election, foreknowledge, predestination, and redemption can only be perceived by realizing that the God of creation is not bound by His own creation. God is not bound by time. God sees past, present, and future all at once. Just because God knows how man will react in life does not mean He makes man act in any way. Therefore, with foreknowledge that is not intrusive, God can elect and predestine those who will trust Him.

XIII. *The Mystery of the Seven Stars and Seven Lampstands (Rev. 1:20)*

The mystery of the seven stars and seven lampstands is referencing the messengers and messages to the seven churches John was instructed to write in Asia Minor. There are seven different locations, congregations, and messages. The messages addressed their existing spiritual conditions and issues within each church. The messages also point to each church representing a period that exhibits a predominant spiritual condition throughout the Church age. The first church was Ephesus that represented the apostolic period. The last church was Laodicea that will represent the apathetic lukewarm church prior to the rapture. To view the mystery as the spiritual condition and sequence of church effectiveness, and ending with Laodicea clearly indicates the Church will not remain on earth during the tribulation.

XIV. Mystery Babylon the Great and the Mystery of the Woman (Rev. 17:5,7)

With the Church removed from the earth, the Holy Spirit no longer restraining evil and Iniquity coming to its pinnacle, a worldwide apostate religion will dominate the nations' leaders and people. The apostacy is represented by a religious whore; the same as Israel was called when she went a-whoring after other gods. The whore will dominate while persecuting and killing Christians. She will be destroyed by the Satanic trinity and the kings that follow the beast, as the beast will require worship of himself as a god.

XV. The Mystery of God Should Be Finished (Rev. 10:7)

The finished mystery of God was purposed through the mystery of His wisdom, not the wisdom of the world. The mystery of His wisdom was hidden from Satan and all intelligent beings. God's purpose for all of His creation was revealed in accordance with His time and place through the prophets. The believer's understanding of the mystery of God begins at creation when God was all-in-all (Father, Son, Holy Spirit). Man sinned and was separated from God. Only God the Son would reveal himself to mankind, as continued provision was made to redeem man with the final act of redemption and justification being Jesus Christ going willingly to the cross to bear the sins of the world. From the time sin entered the world by Adam's disobedience, God has not been all-in-all, illustrated by the Father turning His back on the

Son when Jesus hung on the cross and said, "My God my God, why hast thou forsaken me?" The act of redemption is complete, leaving mankind with the choice to accept or reject what Jesus Christ did on the cross. All of creation waits for God to bring His plan to completion. That will happen when Christ comes again, establishes his kingdom, and puts all enemies under his feet. When Christ has subdued all things and delivers up the kingdom to God the Father and is subject unto the Father, God will again be all-in-all. At that time, the mystery of God will be finished.

Bibliography

Carter, Ian, "Positive and Negative Liberty," *The Stanford Encyclopedia of Philosophy* (Summer 2018 Edition), Edward N. Zalta (ed) https://plato.stanford.edu/archives/sum2018/entries/iberty-positive-negative/

Editors, "History of Israel: Timeline" The Embassy of Israel in South Africa. https://embassies.gov.11/pretoria/AboutIsrael/history/pages/History-Israel-Timeline-OSPX

Grosser, P.E., Halperin, E.G., *Anti-Semitism: Causes and Effects*, New York: Philosophical Library, 1978.

Jamison, Tommy L., "Revelation for the Layperson," Xulon Press, Maitland Florida, 2020.

Kirkland, Bob, *Calvinism: None Dare Call It Heresy*, Lighthouse Trails Publishing, Eureka, Montana, 2018.

Mark, Joshua J., "Israel," *Ancient History Encyclopedia*, https://www.ancient.eu/Israel/.

Riley, Jim L., *Moderate Political Ideologies: Liberalism and Conservatism*, Regis University, Denver, 1990. Jim-riley.org/libcoms.htm. Accessed March 18, 2017.

Strong, James, LL.D., S.T.D., *Exhaustive Concordance of the Bible*. Thomas Nelson Publishers, Nashville, Tennessee, 1990.

The Maccabees/Hasmoneans: History & Overview, https: jewishvirtuallibrary.org:

Vine, W.E., *An Expository Dictionary of New Testament Words with their Precise Meanings for English Readers*, (Fleming H. Revell Company: Old Tappan, 1966).

Whiston, William, *The Works of Flavius Josephus, Book VI, Chapter IX*, Broadman Press Nashville, Tennessee. April, 1978.

References

Holy Bible, Authorized King James Version, The Scofield Study Bible, editor C.I. Scofield, DD, Oxford University Press, Inc. New York, 1996.

Interlinear GreekEnglish New Testament, Authorized King James Version, editor George Ricker Berry, Baker Book House, Grand Rapids Michigan, 1981.

CPSIA information can be obtained
at www.ICGtesting.com
Printed in the USA
LVHW051138120122
708210LV00013B/475